"What Happened to You?"

"What Happened to You?"

WRITING BY DISABLED WOMEN

EDITED BY LOIS KEITH

THE NEW PRESS NEW YORK

LIBRARY OF CONGRESS CATALOG CARD NUMBER 96-67347
ISBN 1-56584-025-9 (HC)
ISBN 1-56584-280-4 (PB)

Originally published in 1994 by The Women's Press, a member
of the Namara Group, 34, Great Sutton Street, London EC1V 0DX
Published in the United States by The New Press, New York
Distributed by W. W. Norton & Company, Inc., New York

*Established in 1990 as a major alternative to the large, commercial publishing houses,
The New Press is a full-scale nonprofit American book publisher outside of the
university presses. The Press is operated editorially in the public interest, rather than
for private gain; it is committed to publishing in innovative ways works
of educational, cultural, and community value that, despite their intellectual merits,
might not normally be commercially viable. The New Press's editorial offices
are located at the City University of New York.*

Printed in the United States of America

9 8 7 6 5 4 3 2 1

To Colin, for helping to make things possible

Contents

"What Happened to You?"

Foreword

To the thirty-six women who come alive in *"What Happened to You?"*, we owe a debt of immeasurable gratitude. The contributors wrote from a variety of perspectives, sometimes painful, sometimes joyful, but always with a profound reverence for self-respect, personal choice, and quality of life. Although they reside in Great Britain, their stories will resonate for all of us, and will have universal appeal throughout the world.

Reading this book has allowed me to reflect on my own disability, and encouraged me to think about our national understanding of what it means to live with a disability. Since 1972, I have traveled with, worked with, and drawn strength from disabled people throughout the world. That year, my brother Ricky and I attended the worldwide Paralympic Games in Heidelberg, Germany. Here for the first time I met disabled people from all over the world, many of them working to improve conditions for disabled people in their home countries.

I was discovering that Europeans already received government assistance—to make homes wheelchair accessible, for instance, or to obtain durable medical equipment—that we in the United States were just beginning to imagine. The European norm of government-supported child care, universal health care, and assistance to the disabled norm makes the lives of disabled Europeans much easier than those of their American counterparts. Nowhere did I see or hear about disabled people living at the level of poverty that was common among the disabled in the United States.

At the same time, I realized that the civil rights movement in our country had paved the way for the disabled community to demand and win our rights. All around us in the 1960s and 1970s in America, we saw emerging political movements gaining momentum, but disabled people were too often being hidden from view, trotted out for annual telethons where viewers were asked to give money to cure or to prevent our disabilities. Real change in the everyday lives of disabled people came not from such gala events, but from the dedication of tireless advocates and activists who have worked—and are still working—to break down the box in which much of the world has dictated we must live. None of this has been easy, and it is by no means finished, but we have proved that it is possible.

Of paramount importance in this continuing struggle are books such as *"What Happened to You?"* Within the past twenty years, we have begun to see literature written by disabled people appear in the popular press. Many of these books have helped to contribute to the growing success of our movement, by opening our eyes, nourishing our spirits, and letting us laugh or howl at experiences we all share. What is particularly wonderful about this book is that all the pieces are written by disabled women. With much of what we have seen and learned about disabled people focused on men with disabilities, there is a real need for disabled women to be able to come together and share our unique experiences. I do believe that the experiences of disabled women, like those of women without disabilities, are different from those of disabled men. As disabled women, we have been starved for role models. This book provides them in spades.

I hope this book will reach people outside of the disabled community as well. If we are ever going to change our country, we need not only to empower ourselves, but also to challenge the minds and hearts of people all across the country regarding our capabilities and the contributions we can make to our local and global communities. This book allows all of us—whether disabled or non-disabled, male or female, old or young—to gather new insights into the hearts and minds of disabled women. I hope you learn from it and take pleasure from it as I did.

JUDITH HEUMANN

Assistant Secretary for Special Education
and Rehabilitative Services,
United States Department of Education
Washington, D.C.

Acknowledgements

I would like to thank all the contributors to this book for their work and patience. I received support from many friends, and Jenny Morris and Joanna Owen were a great help in getting me started. Kathy Gale at The Women's Press was always a most enthusiastic supporter, and her editorial skills and attention to detail were a great help to me. One sadness is that my father, Herbie Keith, died of cancer in 1992, three years after my mother, Hilda. Their love and support were constants in my life and I would have liked them to see this book.

A special thank you goes to my daughters, Rachel and Miriam, for their love, hugs and tea-making skills.

Permissions

The editor would like to thank Alan Holden for permission to reprint 'Along the lane . . .' and 'Pain Teaches Nothing' by Molly Holden, previously published in *Molly Holden, Selected Poems*, Carcanet Press Ltd. Copyright © Alan Holden, 1987.

Some of the contributions to *Mustn't Grumble* have previously been published as follows: 'Bitter and Twisted' and 'Our Friendship Is Mellowed to a Whisper, Sister' by Aspen, 'Shopping' by Caroline Ball and 'For Those Not Yet Angry' by Jennifer Hoskins appeared in *Rainbows in the Ice: Poetry by Disabled Writers* published by Crocus Books, 1992; 'Loss' by Ann Macfarlane, 'To a Deaf Child' by Dorothy Miles and 'Do Unto Others' by Janice Pink were originally published in *Disability Arts in London* magazine; 'Disability' by Jenni Meredith and 'Sight' by Kaite O'Reilly were previously published in *DAM* (Disability Arts Magazine), 10 Wood Lane, Great Coates, Grimsby DN37 9NH; and 'Tomorrow I'm Going to Rewrite the English Language' appeared in *Able Lives*, edited by Jenny Morris, first published by The Women's Press Ltd, 1989.

Introduction

In 1985, I was going about my business as a thirty-five year old woman with a part-time job in educational research, two very young daughters, a much-loved partner of many years and a typical London three-storey Victorian house, when my life took a completely different course. I was hit by a speeding motorist. Overnight I became a wheelchair user, paralysed from the chest down.

It took a year or so to sort out the practical details of our lives, and looking back on it now, I'm not exactly sure how we managed to survive it all. During this time I was in and out of hospital having various bits of me repaired; we fought and won a legal case for compensation; planned where and how we would live in the future; and fought battles about employment. Hardest of all of these was having to cope with living in a house built on five different levels, with a toddler and a baby who was just learning to walk.

Towards the end of 1986, we moved into an accessible flat and began to settle down to a new way of living. For more or less the first time in my life, I began to take pleasure in doing the things that women conventionally do, the cooking, washing up, taking the warm clothes out of the dryer and folding them up neatly. I looked after my children, bathed them and put them to bed, took them to the park on my electric scooter. Small, intense pleasures. After two years I had re-learnt how to drive, enrolled my elder daughter at school and gone back to work.

During this time, I was lucky to have the continued support of my husband Colin, my parents and friends. I have heard many stories from newly disabled people of how friends stop phoning, cross the road when they see you coming, walk out of parties through one door whilst you wheel in through another. My friends did not desert me, they kept in touch, wanted to come and see me, offered support and love.

But there were things that I couldn't or didn't want to talk to them about. After my accident, I found that the beliefs which we had always shared about equality and justice were not enough to help me understand the complicated and sometimes hostile world in which I now found myself as a disabled person. As someone who cared about oppression and who had spent much time campaigning on issues of gender and race in my work in education, these were things I should have known about but didn't. As I began to make sense of the different world I now seemed to inhabit, I found that while I could describe and explain my new life to my friends if I wanted, I couldn't learn about it from them. Sometimes I didn't want to talk about these new experiences and sometimes when I did, they found it hard to listen. I realised that to survive and make sense of my new life, I had to find the support of people like myself. I had to become a member of a new community.

Through meeting other disabled women, talking in the way women do talk when they are together and reading what little there was by disabled writers, I began to understand that my inability to be a full part of this society was not, in fact, my fault. Important things were made inaccessible to me, not because of my inability to walk, but because of laws and regulations which were designed to shut me out. I was now living in a society which had permission to exclude me from things I had grown to consider my right, like access to public buildings, employment, or just being able to go to the cinema of my choice on a Saturday night. I had now become someone people felt sorry for, someone who could be approached by total strangers in public places and asked intrusive questions. At work, people who I had campaigned with on equal opportunities issues now suggested that I might like to think about applying for early retirement.

Like many of the contributors to this book, I found that an

important way to deal with these new experiences was to write about them. In those earliest days, my writing was about the personal pain and loss I felt about the changes to my body and my fear at the loss of privacy and independence. Later, when I learnt that life was going to be good after all, I began to try to make sense of the society I lived in, the prejudice and fear of disability, the encounters with strangers that unsettled and disturbed me, and the images of myself I met through books I had grown up with. I was concerned, too, with the current popular debate about the rights and needs of those who 'cared for' disabled people, which somehow left me out altogether. Where was my position in this world as a disabled woman, how was I to make sense of it all and come through it, confident and strong?

I needed to be able to 'name' these experiences in order to be able to handle them and I wanted to hear what other disabled women were thinking and feeling. The disability movement, like every group struggling to make its voice heard, needs its own literature and there was remarkably little published writing by disabled women. I decided to fill the gap.

Plucking up courage, I rang up one or two publishers to talk about the idea. Receiving the predictable brush-off, I felt dejected. Then, in 1992, I finally got my act together and sent a detailed proposal to The Women's Press (a feminist press based in London), together with a small collection of writing by people I had worked with in writing groups. They were impressed with the power and originality of this writing and we began to do business.

Having a contract at this early stage gave me the confidence to ask women to send me their work. By this time I had developed a small network of disabled women friends who were, and still are, vital to me. I asked for the names of women they knew who were writing. I put announcements in the columns of Women's Pages in the national press, and in disability newspapers and magazines, which were then picked up by local networks. Women told friends about it and workshop leaders ran writing groups based on ideas I had put in my 'flyer'.

The manuscripts began to arrive, and continued to do so for more than a year. (I miss that hopeful thud through my letterbox now that contributions have stopped coming!) It was hard to make any decisions at first and I spent some time feeling rather overwhelmed by the pile of recycled brown envelopes on my desk. Putting together an anthology is an organic process – it begins to take shape once you have a core of pieces which you know will be included. Once I had overcome this difficult initial stage, I began to enjoy it.

One of the great delights of this anthology turned out to be the dialogue which developed between myself and the contributors. Only a few of the pieces in this book appear exactly as they did when they first arrived on my doormat. I responded to many of them with comments and suggestions, and authors replied agreeing or disagreeing. Our correspondence took up a lot of time but I learned a great deal from it and I hope they did too. I built up an enormous file of letters which explored a very wide range of issues about writing and disability. Our letters discussed literary matters of form and style, but they are also about the whole business of impairment and illness, passivity and strength. They explored ideas about whether it was possible to be proud of being disabled when all your energy was sapped by illness or pain and what words we could use to describe our personal journey and our encounters with the world. These letters are a fascinating record of the editorial process and they show the misunderstandings as well as the mutual support that can take place between editor and writer. They add an extra dimension to the voices in this book and since I obviously couldn't include them all, I chose to include the correspondence between myself and three very different writers. They appear in an appendix at the end.

Decisions about what to include in an anthology necessarily include decisions about what to reject. I looked again at the anthologies of women's writing I had on my shelf and although I discovered lots of comments just like mine about how full the mailboxes were, I found nothing about the flip side of selecting work for inclusion. This silence isn't surprising. Choosing work for an anthology is a great pleasure but rejecting it can be difficult and painful. Sometimes it was quite easy – the four-stanza poem I received from a nurse entitled 'Three Cheers for Volunteers' was speedily returned and I read many pieces of interesting writing which were nothing to do with the experience of being disabled – but mostly it was hard.

My criteria for inclusion were varied. I wanted material which was creative and original in style and form as well as pieces which were simple and direct. I looked for contributions from women from a wide variety of backgrounds and ages, and with different impairments and experiences. I wanted work which dealt with the most private aspects of our lives, and writing which moved on from this point to explore personal and political change for disabled people. I had to reject a lot of good things.

Who is this book for? Originally it was for me, and perhaps that isn't a bad place to start. I wanted, indeed needed, to hear other disabled women describe and explain their lives. I knew that however different they were, we would share many of the same experiences of exclusion and prejudice because of the barriers we all faced. I also wanted to understand more about disabled women whose impairment and physical experiences were different from my own, but who were part of my world.

At the same time, I believe that this anthology is about universal experience. Women will instinctively recognise some of the main themes of this book – how fragile our grasp of independence can be and how we have to fight to define it for ourselves; how difficult things can be for those of us who are not 5 feet 6 inches tall, thin and blonde, with complete working parts; how tough and isolating it is to live with pain or illness; how easy it is for us to accept other people's view of ourselves as second-class citizens, and why we must fight to reject such definitions. These are things we all share. I believe that the quality of writing in this anthology, the energy and the originality of the pieces and the hard and challenging subjects that are dealt with here, mean that this book will be read, understood and valued by many people.

This book does not follow a 'party line'. A wide range of

views and experiences are included and I haven't felt the need to 'agree' with all the contributors. As well as women who are political about being disabled, there is also writing by women who reject the pressures they feel imposed on them to take some sort of 'correct' view.

I also decided that it was important to include writing by women who are ill rather than disabled, even though for many years disabled people have been fighting the stereotypical view of ourselves as weak and sick – the 'medical model'. A friend who has been disabled all her adult life wrote to me at the start of this project with this concern.

> One thing I am not one hundred per cent sure about, and I know this is a purely personal hunch, is that it is going to be an anthology of writing by disabled women and women with disabling illnesses. It seems to me, to put it in its most simplistic form, that the experiences of someone like me are fundamentally different from those of a woman who is, for example, dying of cancer. I know that we have many things in common, feelings of frustration, anger, pain, oppression from those who don't understand, but also there are differences. I know my condition is stable and that I'm not going to die soon. At a time when many disabled women are trying to counter the myth that disability equals illness, I worry that it may be too much to take on this extra dimension. Perhaps it is more important for us to get a more general understanding and awareness of how we feel and how we want to be defined. Once that has been achieved and once we have gained strength and recognition by 'naming' ourselves, then we can go on to ally ourselves with women who are ill and explore ways in which we are similarly oppressed.

I understand this concern, but it seems to me that our experiences are on a continuum. We are not either ill or healthy, weak or strong. Some of us are stable and well, others are just acquiring conditions which may be difficult and frightening. Some disabled women are living strong lives but have physical conditions which are progressive and have to deal with this loss as part of their everyday lives. I feel that there are enough hierarchies created for us from outside – the benefits system, decisions about who deserves to be rehoused or receive a proper education, whose lives are worth living – without us creating new hierarchies for ourselves.

It *is* important to try to counteract the popular view of ourselves as sick, tragic figures, but if we do this by denying the realities of our lives, which are sometimes painful and sad, we are just swopping the 'tragic but brave' model the world is so fond of for another kind of dangerous myth in which we must always be fighters. Apart from anything else, this is a very male way to look at the world.

An important part of becoming strong comes from being able to acknowledge, for ourselves, the physical and emotional pain and the loss of independence and status which can be part of our experience. Ann Macfarlane, a contributor to this book and a long-term disability campaigner, has written elsewhere:

> It is, of course, important to have a political perspective, to know your rights and be able to argue your case, but during this process you have to stay very close to the pain. Sometimes the pain has been too much and I've had to push it away and put on the 'supercrip' role. Now I've grown through that too and I believe that some of my strength comes from that weakness.

Many of the women writing in this book are ruthlessly honest about how it hurts to always have to struggle for our right to a place in this world. But as well as the pain, there is warmth and humour in the writing here and for many readers there will be the sigh of relief that comes when you recognise that you are not alone, that other women have shared your experiences and felt as you do.

This book isn't arranged in themes or subjects. When I first put the proposal together, I imagined that it would be possible to arrange the contributions into sections that showed a process of development such as loss, growing, changing, and moving on. But as I began to read the stories, personal accounts and poems that came in, I realised that this was impossible. The questions that disabled women ask are complicated and profound and the answers challenge us all. The writing in this book cannot be put into simple categories because each piece takes us on its own journey.

The title *"What Happened to You?"* comes from a very funny piece by Janice Pink in which she tells us her whole life story in just a few pages. I didn't want to call this book something new-agey like *Flying Over the Hurdles* (or *One Foot on the Pedestal* as it became affectionately known in my household) or something that might be interpreted as "worthy" like *Strong and Proud* even though that's what we are. The question will be instantly recognizable to disabled people and the irony of it makes me smile.

Janice begins her piece, "What Happened to You?" Well, that's what people ask you. Then they ask if it was an accident, sniffing for BLOOD. Sometimes I tell them I got hit on the head by a meteorite. This question, along with "What's wrong with you then?" and "Are you going to get better?" is asked all the time by well-meaning and sometimes not so well-meaning strangers and is a particular feature of the lives of those of us who have visible impairments.

It's hard to get our responses right. If we tell people to mind their own business we are accused of being rude and bitter. If we decide to answer (assuming something happened—it may be that we were just born into our bodies) we are allowing others to invade our privacy and our sense of ourselves. Even if we manage to find a brilliant and funny riposte, we're still left feeling that we are the ones who have overreacted or been oversensitive. ("I was just asking. No need to be like that.") For disabled women, learning how to deal with the questions people ask us and talking about them when we are together is a kind of survival strategy. By sharing our experiences we work things out and carry on.

This book was first published under the title, *Mustn't Grumble*, which is the name of a piece by Roz Rushworth, but my American publishers thought that this expression was just too British and its particular humor might not appeal to U.S. readers. *Mustn't Grumble* is what women say to each other when what they really want to do is have a good moan about things which are making them feel fed up. On the other hand, as Roz said to me, it's also a way of shutting up people who assume that our lives are a miserable lot but actually know nothing about us. *"What Happened to* You?*"* is the other side of this same coin. When Roz is faced with the kind of people who ask this question, "Mustn't Grumble" is her polite way of saying, "Mind your own business!"

The title *"What Happened to* You?*"* is above all, ironic. As someone once said, "Irony is to experience what salt is to soup. It is flavor, it is nuance." This book is part of the coming out of disable women writers, but it is not writing that just slaps our experiences down on the table like a wet herring for others to look at. It is self-critical, self-aware writing that says: "You might choose to see me as passive and quiet, or bitter and twisted, but here are the ways I am fighting back. This is how *I* see things, this is how *I* choose to describe them." The terrible isolation experienced by some of us, our protective devices and our lack of power, often keep us hidden from the world, and I am very grateful to all the women who were willing to put their personal and private voices into print.

LOIS KEITH
London, December 1995

PART ONE

Ellie O'Sullivan

The Visit

How funny, I think, to be sitting here, in my home, with this woman from Social Services sitting opposite. She tells me what I already know, I have been referred by the Occupational Therapy Department. Funny name that – Occupational Therapy. I thought they'd made a mistake when they first sent me to Occupational Therapy, it sounded altogether inappropriate, much too active. Too Occupational really.

How will she grade me, I wonder? She might think I've got her here under false pretences. Maybe I have. I don't know.

I look over at Charlotte to see what sense she is making of it all. She smiles, but I can tell she is anxious.

'I will start by asking you some routine questions, Mrs . . .'

I am struck by the archaism of that 'Mrs'. Nobody calls me Mrs. I'm not a Mrs. Definitely not a Mrs.

I come back to her, alerted by a change of tone, a note of firmness mixed with embarrassment.

'. . . and your answers must be truthful. I will ask you to sign a form at the end of the interview confirming as much. Do you understand?'

I nod eagerly at the woman, anxious to show willing, feeling childish in front of this officialdom, in my house, in front of my child.

Charlotte sits. Watching.

'Right,' the woman says, not unkindly. 'Can we start with your name?'

Instantly I am muddled. Do I give my married name, just in case they should decide that I have deceived them? Or do I give the name I go by, my maiden name? I give my maiden name – O'Sullivan.

'And your christian name?'

More muddle. The name I was christened with, Eileen, the one I grew up with, isn't me. Not any more. But it is my official name, the one used in my medical records – I give it, feeling strange.

And Charlotte. It will seem strange to her too, to hear her mother identify herself by this name, making me strange to her as well. I want to tell her to find something to do but don't feel able.

'Your address?'

I relax. So much easier, so much easier. A number. A street name. Nothing to judge. Nothing to question.

I catch Charlotte's eye. I smile. We'll have a laugh about it later. She picks up a book. This isn't too bad, I think.

I notice the women's accent for the first time. Irish, I think. Hope. Will that make her softer on me? Harder? And what about my lack of accent? Will she realise that I am Irish? Was Irish? Am Irish? The name should tell her. Maybe she'll think it's my husband's, not mine. In any case maybe she prefers no accent. Less vulnerable.

'Date of birth?'

I answer. Will she be surprised? Will she think I look younger? No surprise. I feel tired.

'Okay', smiles the woman. 'I understand you're suffering from rheumatoid arthritis and it's causing you problems, is that right?'

'Yes', I say.

I'm sure she thinks I should be able to manage. I'm sure she thinks that. She probably sees people who are much worse than me. She probably thinks I'm a fraud, a malingerer. Someone trying to get something for nothing. I don't look like someone who needs help. People are always saying how amazed they are at how I manage. I'm amazed at their amazement. Why wouldn't I be able to manage? – I'm not that bad.

I look across at Charlotte, glad that she is absorbed in her book.

'Okay,' says the woman, 'what we need to do is decide which home aids will best help you to cope with your disability. We'll proceed room by room, that way we should avoid leaving anything out. So, we'll start with the sitting room. Is there anything we could do to make things easier for you here?'

I look around the sitting room, relieved that it is looking so tidy. Pleasant really. 'No', I say. 'I think I'm okay here.'

'What about the settee?' she says, looking doubtful. 'Doesn't that cause you problems? It looks a bit low to me.'

Gosh, I think, how clever of her to know that, to know that it is awkward, difficult to get up from.

'Well,' I say, not sure. 'I can't get up directly but with a bit of manoeuvring it's not too bad.'

I want her to know that I am resourceful, that I am trying. Not a fraud.

'Well,' she says, 'we could have the settee heightened. Of course the settee won't look so nice, but it will make things easier.

I agree, relieved, tempted by the prospect of being able to rise more easily, not having to twist so awkwardly, not having to search out ways to avoid getting up. Not having to wait for Charlotte or Pete to move so that I can ask them to get me this or that, just to avoid the awkwardness. Maybe it would be easier if the settee were raised.

How wonderful, I think, how wonderful that such things are still possible, even with the cuts. It is extraordinary that a department exists somewhere devoted exclusively to making life easier for someone like me.

I like her voice, her soft familiar accent.

'What about the armchair?'

'Oh, that's fine,' I say firmly, glad that I don't need help on this. 'It's already nice and high.'

Charlotte is reading and I feel better.

'And the kitchen,' says the woman from Social Services, 'what about the kitchen?'

'I'm fine there,' I say. 'My husband does the cooking.'

'What, all of it?' She looks sceptical.

'Yes,' I say, defensively. 'My husband likes cooking. He's a very good cook.'

I bet she thinks I'm a monster. She probably thinks I'm a real monster.

'What happens when he is not here?'

I think of the times when the arthritis is bad, when I struggle to cut the bread or open a tin. I want to tell her, though, that I make films – that I can do lots of things, lots of things.

'It's all right,' I say, 'but I suppose I do have some difficulty.'

'Fine,' she says, adding to her list. 'I'll order some kitchen aids, it'll make things easier.'

It might make things easier, I think. It would be nice to know I needn't worry, that I can do things without Pete.

'What about the stairs?'

'So long as I take it steady I think I'm all right,' I say.

'Are you sure?' she says. 'They look rather awkward to me. It wouldn't hurt to put a few strategic rails in, just in case.'

I see the stairs and am reminded of how many times I have imagined falling.

I hope Charlotte is still reading.

'That would be nice,' I say. 'It would make things easier.'

'The bedroom?'

'Everything is fine there,' I say, 'absolutely fine, no problems.'

'And the bathroom?'

I feel hot, the room is too hot.

I must tell her about the bath.

If only Charlotte weren't here. If only she'd go downstairs. If only someone would ring for her, because I have to tell about the business of the bath.

I must tell the woman about how when Pete helps me out of the bath I am afraid. I am afraid that he will damage himself. It is an awkward movement bending to lift someone out of a bath and I am afraid I will be too heavy for him and that he will fall and I will fall with him. But I am also afraid when I struggle alone. My legs will not do what is necessary and I can no longer remember how they ever did. So I am afraid as I lever myself up on to the back of the bath.

And I have another fear – I remember the time sitting in the bath. I am ready to get out but I cannot. I call for Pete but he cannot hear me. I call and call until I am afraid that I shall never be heard. And this makes me so afraid that I stop calling. And I start to cry and I cannot stop. Pete comes and he is overwhelmed with remorse because he did not hear. And my daughter comes and sees her mother in the bath, unable to get out, and she cries with shock and fear.

So I must tell this woman about the problem of the bath. But I want my daughter to go downstairs. I don't want her to see how much I need something to get me in and out of the bath without being afraid. But I know that the bath chair, which is what I need, is a costly item and I must make my case convincing, so I must tell this woman. But my child is here and I don't want her to know how helpless I am. But I need the bath chair because I am so afraid of falling, falling and not being heard.

I know that Charlotte is no longer reading, that she is listening as I tell this stranger about my helplessness. I want to turn to her, to tell her that it is only this one thing, that she needn't worry. But I can't.

I finish and I see the woman before me soft with sympathy.

'Don't worry,' she says kindly, 'we'll get the chair installed as quickly as possible.'

I do not look at Charlotte. I want to ask her forgiveness. I want to tell her how ashamed I am, that she needn't worry, that I am okay.

But she is already moving towards me, her arms encircling my legs, reassuring me, protecting me.

I look down at my hands, the swelling clearly visible, the bones distorted. I rise to show the woman out. I do so awkwardly and full of pain.

Molly Holden

Pain Teaches Nothing

Pain teaches nothing except
the pure beauty of relief from pain,
eyes looking easily about once more,
the breath drawn slow again.

Nothing but pain matters while
it is present; music, sunlight,
the fate of children, are of no
consequence. Only the coming night

is extra agony, the body only fears
dark, silence, centuries of hours;
and even morning brings no interest
in food, warmth, flowers.

Pain teaches nothing except
the pure beauty of relief from pain,
– quiet sleep at last, and, on waking,
the spirit articulate again.

Kaite O'Reilly

Sight

In the heated classroom, prickling with infant sweat and chalk powder, a child at the back squints her eyes tortuously. The teacher holds up a turquoise globe, smilingly declaring the world to be round.

Round?

The child fidgets, watching the revolving ball, the pinks and yellows of land merging with the blue for sea.

Round?

She checks her neighbour for kindred disbelief, but finds him easy and uncompromised, teeth gnawing nail distractedly.

Round? No, it was flat, a screen without dimension.

Round?

The teacher, sensing heresy, says again that the world is round – in fact spherical – and are there any questions?

The child shakes her head, opening her atlas to page nine, remaining silent. Slowly, a bloom of fear unfurls within.

The playground.

'Blind old Betty
        Couldn't find the jetty
        And fell flat into the water.'

Skipping girls, running races, goal posts marked with woollen jumpers.

'Who wants a game of Batman and Robin?'

'Who'll play tig?'

'Rounders?'

She steps forward hopefully as another says, 'Not her, she's rubbish. Can't catch or hit the ball or anything. She's useless.'

The children jeer, their catching-ball hands resting smugly on each other's shoulders. She shrugs. Aims to kick a stone and misses. Pretends to do so deliberately, and starts an improvised soft shoe shuffle. They snigger. She strolls away, haughty and noncommittal. Already she has learnt the first lesson. Never let the enemy know you are hurting. Never let them know you're not happiest alone.

Years pass. Their round, her flat world continues to emerge in marked difference.

She finds she can't draw cubes and as a result is placed in the remedial class. There she privately tutors her peers whilst learning how to draw six sides without understanding the effect.

Her birthday comes. A jocular older brother takes her to see *Jaws 3* in living technovision.

She sits in the auditorium, cardboard spectacles perched on her nose, watching the screen in half red, half green, puzzling whilst all around her scream and dodge. She finds the experience disappointing and tells her brother so, regretting it immediately.

'Didn't you see the big fish leap out from the screen?'

She shakes her head in mystification, in envy. He doesn't believe her, deciding she is just trying to be remarkable.

They walk home in silence.

Months pass and her stick insect body creates contortions beneath her hands. She weighs the growing breasts in each palm and earns a scurrilous reputation from trying to do similar with a girl in the changing rooms.

'I was only trying to see', she explains to the thin-lipped Games Mistress. 'I can't look without touch. Isn't everybody the same?'

She is told to keep her dirty opinions and hands to herself.

She shuffles into the emptying showers, eyes trained on the floor. Another lesson is learnt. She must wear blinkers in their rounded world.

Exams pass and with them the first stage of her innocence.

She finds a boy dawdling behind after the End of School Party and allows him to accompany her home. She is surprised when, in a bus shelter, he takes her hands and places them on his face.

His features unfold beneath her touch, becoming extra-ordinary and multi-faceted. She traces the outline of his skull, dipping into the hollows of his eye sockets, the even bite of teeth above his jaw.

She thinks it must be love. Or do all balloon faces sculpt so beneath the hand? She realises he is beautiful; the flat roundness she sees carves into shapes and irregularities with her hand. She marvels, fingers gliding over the bones beneath the skin's surface. He grows embarrassed. A tension builds, soothed by the first kiss which she enthusiastically administers. A sad kiss, her enthusiasm born of gratitude.

But at least she has learnt something. People resemble not what she sees, but what she feels.

Winter follows autumn and the years pass. The sense of being odd moulds into her character; she presents a public mask to their tangible world.

She is rounded, now, in touch, but angular in her looking-glass. She dons the pleated party dress, shamefaced at the plunging neckline. Her body curves in relief like mountains, like the stone angel on her grandfather's grave.

She arrives early at the church Christmas disco, so piously visits Our Lady's Chapel. The candles echo along the walls, quivering like moth wings upon the Virgin's face. She watches the figure in blue shimmering, glowing, made heady by the scent of incense.

Our Lady moves and the alabaster lips smile down on her. She tingles. Our Lady blinks earthwards, the stone robe flowing into fabric. She reaches up, knowing she has been blessed with vision. The candles flicker; Our Lady breathes. Consumed with vocation her fingers glide along the moving breasts, finding them cold and inanimate beneath her touch. She is confused, her twin telling senses contradictory, making mockery. She climbs up on to the statue's ledge, clutching at the lungs beneath the stone. Do they move or not? Is this a calling or hallucination?

The priest roars out and she falls on to concrete and into scandal. She is requested never to attend the church again. Her family, briefly, disown her. She learns another lesson. Her sight is maverick, theirs restricted. She decides to become gnostic and veer away from their seeing world.

More time passes and womanhood settles more easily on her bones. She is given the reputation of a sphinx owing to her wandering, unfocused eyes. Certain men become infatuated, realising they will never stare deeply into both eyes at once. She smiles, one eye watching them, the other looking at something invisible, just beyond their shoulder, always out of reach. They find it intoxicating, something of a challenge. The hated 'squinty-googie' eyes of childhood suddenly become an aphrodisiac.

She thinks she prefers their former status and finds men's attraction to her inordinately silly.

Meanwhile she has grown accustomed to her playful, vicious sight. She meditates briefly on others' ability to gauge depth and height and walk through a crowd without continual bruise-making collisions.

An optician examines her eyes and finds her seeing power excellent. She shrugs, believing his diagnosis of inherited clumsiness or PMS. She ignores the headaches, the flashing lights, the frequent migraines, and sets off alarms in Rome when fingering Michelangelo's David, discovering the famous penis is even smaller in touch than sight.

Then the blindness comes, swooping down upon her. Her fascinating eyes go out, leaving her trembling in an alien room, rank with the metallic cleanliness of scalpels.

The experts come and shake their heads, using dictionary terms she can no longer look up. She asks their opinion in laywoman's words and they laugh, calling her a feminist, and 'keep that chin up'.

Her eyes ache. She touches the lids tenderly, remembering the detail of whorled skin on her fingertips, the asymmetrical dart of her eyes in the mirror.

She finds her walk changes, no longer jerky and chin-angled, cocky as a hen, but serene and careful, her ears leading the way.

The trolley comes for her mid-morning and returns her mid-afternoon. She struggles up from the anaesthetic, believing it to be night but for the sunbeams heating her skin beneath the bedclothes.

Relations come and visit, their voices alien and squawkish in the little black room: the forced jauntiness repulsive, ricocheting about her head, until they leave, whispering in funereal undertones.

A young nurse suggests she learns braille and the fear, seeded in the long-distant classroom, unfurls more threateningly inside.

She begins to recollect the spinning globe in the faraway geography class, her unpopularity with her ball-catching friends.

She recalls her delightfully malicious sight, playing tricks on her, offering visions, mirages, hallucinations. Those moving statues, animated objects; her sight which breathed life into dead, never-living things. Her wonder of discovery – that mountains *do* exist, they are not painted shapes on a theatrical backdrop; that physical realisation of distance – like walking into a photograph, she can move, move fluidly within a flat picture, strolling through an apparent dead-end screen.

She begins to understand her outsider sensibility, the jigsaw puzzle which looked right but never fitted. The calamitous, careless nicknames. The broken test-tubes in the science lab. The spilt wine at dinner parties. The infusion of embarrassment, her self-loathing at never being able to do anything 'right'.

She absorbs all this as she lies in blackout, waiting for the bandages to be removed. Lying with gritted teeth, fuming at the tedious predictability of it all. Why had no one realised? She had been misdiagnosed all her life. Why had no one listened? She was misunderstood and maligned.

Her bloom of fear snaps shut, replaced by an unretractable rage.

Then, as suddenly as it left, her sight returns home. She greets it as the prodigal daughter, embracing her flat world with a terrible tenderness.

She is wiser now and contemptuous, watching her family seize the medical term. They recount her past idiosyncrasies, smiling inanely, redefining her with the official label.

'It's only because you're partially sighted!'

She listens to them with her sphynx-like grin. She has learnt her last lesson. She knows 'only' has nothing to do with it.

Mary Duffy

Making Choices

somebody's daughter
CHILD

i am your daughter.
i was born in your double bed.
you thought i was half bird
that i had wings.

afterwards you thought
god had chosen you specially for me,
and you were going to love me so much
it wouldn't make any difference.

they blamed it on sputnik and the russians and gave me
artificial arms
when i was eight months old.
they came out of the airing cupboard every morning
to help me develop a body image that included arms
while we all waited for technology to catch up.

i am to be discouraged from using my feet,
and 'bionic' limbs arrive when i am five years old.
they are big heavy hooks
powered by gas cylinders
and you send them back after two weeks.

with them go all attempts
to make my body conform.

my own
WOMAN

i am growing up,
and you think that i will never go away,
that i will always live with you
be washed and dressed by you
the perfect offspring who never leaves the nest.

you teach me to be independent,
to be strong,
to have my own opinions,
to earn my own living.
neither of us knows
that one day i will dress and wash myself
and live independently.

but i haven't been programmed or conditioned
to be anybody's wife,
lover,
or mother,
you didn't teach me to serve anybody,
to wash and peel potatoes.

you appreciate my intelligence,
creativity, wit, sharpness
and humour.
you call me máire cock
by refusing to inoculate me against rubella,
you ignore my sexuality.

sisters
LOVE

you accused me of always letting you down
just when you needed me most,
and i made you smile and forget your anger
by crooning
'you always hurt the one you love,
the one you shouldn't hurt at all.'

for me, loving you is unconditional
and it shouldn't hurt.
you're my oldest friend, my nearest and dearest,
my childhood, adulthood, past and present.
you are funny,
warm and indomitable.

for me loving you is about letting go
the fear of being hurt,
vulnerable and powerless.
it is about defending my own space and saying no.
it is about forgiveness
and about letting go the feeling
of being responsible for your happiness.

sisters
DEPENDENCE

until i was seventeen
i depended on you
to bring me to the toilet
every day of my life.
it gave you power.
power to care,
control,
manipulate, hurt,
and humiliate.

one hot summer's day i pissed in the school yard
because you would not bring me to the toilet.
i felt terrible despair
and anger,
as the steam rose from my urine
trickling towards the gutter.

today i do not understand,
why i did not break the cycle
and simply ask someone else to help me.

WHOLE

my grannie pulls and strokes,
squeezes and squashes
with love and determination,
to make my little hand grow.
her massaging comes after a long day
hidden
in its hard plastic armour,
sweaty, unused, unseen, sticky.

my fingers,
now curled and bent beneath my breast,
remember her touch.
why don't you leave her the way god left her?
she always asked.

my very first memory,
along with falling
always headlong
and later learning to twist and fall
and hold my head up
and burst my ribs instead of my brains,

is of lying in bed
alongside my grannie.
she scratches my crotch
when i ask.
she calls it my Mogie.

someone else scratches me now.

HOLE

i am twelve years old
i know i am not expected to have children.
i don't know how i know, i just do.
nobody ever said anything:
its probably what they didn't say
that made the difference.

will i grow breasts?
will i bleed?

i am twenty two
in art college
making a video
about my birth.
it involves being naked.
the night before i get my period.
i can't make the video wearing sanitary towels
and i can't insert a tampon.

some friends gather round to help.
they try very hard.
they poke and push and prod
but they can't find the hole.
my very worst fear, along with being unlovable.

making choices
DOUBT

for you disability is a shield,
impassable,
a protection from a hostile world.

when we talked about if it were different . . .
you said if you were able bodied
you wouldn't see my sexuality;
you would only feel protective towards me.

and if i were not disabled
you'd feel you couldn't be sure of me
but that you'd feel great about 'bagging a beautiful
    bird'.

you see our disabilities
as a guarantee against rejection,
but you'd prefer
that i were more whole, complete, and beautiful.

making choices
DIGNITY

i am all these things . . .
whole, complete and beautiful.
our disabilities do not guarantee freedom from the fear
of rejection.
disability does not guarantee
allegiance
or protection.

when i leave you it is
because
i accept myself as i am . . .
i don't need to be part of a relationship
that needs
our disabilities
as security
against hurt, pain and anger.
its no place to grow from . . .

'i want to plant my own garden,
decorate my own soul
instead of waiting for someone to bring me flowers
and i learn that i am really strong,
that i really can endure,
that i really have worth.
and i learn
and i learn and i learn
with every goodbye i learn.'*

*from 'After a While' written by a woman, name unknown.

Ruth Bailey

A Tale of a Bubble

A year passed, shrouded in white. In the eternal monotony, my eyes craved colour – the colour of my quilt cover, of another's eyes meeting mine over a glass of wine, the colour of plates waiting to be washed.

The Social Worker visits to discuss the arrangements which must be made so I can make the transition, go from hospital to home – a shower to replace the bath, a monkey pole behind my bed, someone to give me a hand to get up. I am bursting with excitement. No one hints that there's something between the white and the colour. Perhaps they thought I would know. More likely, they thought it was of little consequence.

I see now that my tale began the day the Social Worker visited. To 'discuss' – it was the first of many ordinary words whose meanings were distorted. The Social Worker was a foot-soldier in the vast Army of Those Who Care. Distortion was one of their weapons, expertly used to disguise their power. There could be no discussion, no exchange of ideas, no debate – the Social Worker had only been given one idea, one solution to discharge.

A Home.

Home, without the indefinite article, she could not consider.

A Home. She wrapped it up in packaging made of promises, made of what she conceived as my best interests – a 'temporary measure', 'a halfway house', 'good rehabilitation'. She secured it with that all-purpose string 'lack of resources'. The packaging was designed to appeal to reason, used to cover her powerful powerlessness. She'd like to help, but... She smiled, a sticky, sickly smile.

I shivered. I had visited a Home when barely starting out on life's adventure. I had seen the stripping of souls. A kindly resident had mistaken me for a new inmate – an easy mistake – disabled, I was no different from her. To make me feel welcome, wanted, she offered to teach me how to crochet dishcloths 'for that's the best thing to do all day here'. I was choked by that individual gesture of kindness amidst all the blandness and desolation. I shivered, I was back at Special School, hating the isolation, hating being told to try that bit harder otherwise 'you'll end up in a home'. That threat never failed; so many disabled people are forced to learn it and forced not to forget it. The threat meant surrender of dignity, surrender of control.

I said No. I watched my 'no' dissipate in the wind.

A Home. A building in an inner-city residential street. I entered. I did not move in. Always listen to the jargon, it says more than they want you to know. It was a liberal Home, built in liberal times, built when people still tried to learn from past mistakes. The door was not locked behind me. But a conspiracy of insignificant events ensured I never got away. The phone shared between five, six, or seven people was never free to make those arrangements – book the Dial-A-Ride, check the access, check the time, make the contact. The staff, who were supposedly our arms and legs, supposedly at our beck and call, were rarely available to take us out, were too rigid to say 'Be back anytime and we'll be there to give you the necessary hand.'

So I came and went as best I could. In the local shops, no one asked where I lived. They knew I came from 'that place'. I no longer had the pleasure of being just a stranger, a pleasure as a disabled person I had fought so hard to get. Here, I could not be known for being different, for standing out by always sitting down. No one looked at my face. No one looked at any of our faces. We were all the same, all that was seen to matter about us was that we sat down, down, down. We were enclosed in thick grey walls to separate us from 'the community'. Walls 'the community' cemented with their fear of our differentness, greyness they painted to make our unique selves and our unique souls indistinguishable.

Desperate, I tried to go further, further, away from the Home. I enrolled for classes in subjects I did not know existed, visited libraries when I had a shelf full of beckoning books. I could not escape for sometimes when people asked in casual conversation, where I lived, I felt I had to tell. To lie would have been to betray my fellow residents. But as I told them, I saw them put me beyond the pale. At other times when people asked where I lived, I could not say. I lied. I could not face the confirmation of my lowly status.

No one went out. So no one returned with the pickings of the day – the moments that make lips stretch to a smile, the insignificances with which families, lovers, friends, wash away the stains of the day. When the day was still young we had said to each other everything we wanted to say. There were no fresh supplies of trivia to hide our secret selves behind.

When I arrived I was told I would be sharing 'a flat' with three others. When I arrived the three residents were told I would be moving in. We had never met before, but it had been decided that our disparate lives would collide. Architects, no doubt in cahoots with bureaucrats, divided this Home into six flats. Each flat was constructed from four shoeboxes and a long lace – a corridor which tied together those four shoebox bedrooms with a single bathroom, and which housed a cooker, fridges, spare wheelchairs, and the proverbial kitchen sink. At each tip of the lace, through the never closed doors, was the next flat, identical in every detail to our own. As I sat in my dressing-gown, in the all-purpose thoroughfare, I did not know who would spy me munching Marmite toast. This was the purpose-built container, without living space, that they saw as fit for us.

Our shoebox rooms, not wide enough to allow a wheelchair, our wheelchairs, to turn, had paper-thin walls. Did I let on I heard my neighbour's intimate conversation with her mother, embarrassing her, making her feel diffident? Or did I pretend not to hear, remaining on my guard, slightly aloof, worried I would let something slip? I worried, too, that she faced a similar dilemma. In the continual noise of so many TV sets, so many voices, I tried to recall who owned which sorrow, which joy. I heard too much. All words became the same. I missed the luxury of private sorrow, the joy of a private tear. What was private had been made public. What was made private, hidden behind those thick grey walls, should have been part of the public community. Private, public, like me, became so confused.

It was too hard to get out, too hard to stay in. The air was limited, stale, putrid. I would gasp to take a breath, and someone else's gasp snatched the air. Try again. The same thing happened. Frantic now, not thinking, gasping, coughing, choking, your neighbour, also frantic, also gasping, coughing, choking. I did not care, as I once had cared. I wrestled to take the air from her lips.

Then there were the Care Staff, Strangers in a strange home, whose place it was to do for residents what we could not do for ourselves. When we asked, so they said. We were always waiting. Frustrated. Waiting on the toilet. Humiliated. The Strangers chose – never purposely, no, no – whose wait to lessen first. They identified residents by our intimate physical needs, judged us by how we said we wanted those needs to be met. I felt my self diminish beneath the weight of others judging, defining; I felt my self shrink in the shrinking space. At change of shift, the Stranger leaving handed over information, gossip, prejudice about the residents to the Stranger just arriving; handed over a plate of brushed-up crumbs. Knowing this, I was forced to wonder what they saw, what they said, about me. One day I mistook a Stranger for a friend and dropped an intimate morsel as she slid my sock over my foot. That evening the same intimate morsel, chewed, masticated, was dropped into my mouth by a different stranger as she slid my sock off my foot. Who was friend? Who was foe? I was forced to hold my tongue. As if making pastry, Strangers rubbed and rubbed residents' lives together and shaped us to their own designs.

One day, the sink broke in the sluice, next to the kitchen. We reported it to the Care Staff who reported it to the Head of Home who reported it to the Council, who owned the building, who ran the Home, to care for us. Nothing happened. Tempers rose, with the stench. The rot set in, with the smell. We moaned, amongst ourselves. Only I, the newcomer, was outraged. Only I, the newcomer, had not learnt that apathy was the way the powerless expressed seething anger. I learnt the lesson. Too quickly. To my disgust. Induced apathy, reduced self-worth were insidious weapons used by the Army Who Care to divide us, to prevent their charges attacking. And these were weapons used to divide the Army itself, so as to protect the power of the unseen, unknown Generals.

In a climate of cuts, the Head of Home sat at the kitchen table. The hatched plan was announced. You, and you, and maybe you, moved to another flat. He didn't ask – we were cards waiting to be shuffled. He didn't tell residents there would be no more agency staff. He didn't tell Care Staff that they would be 'asked' to do overtime, 'asked' to cover, to stretch one pair of arms and legs between twice as many residents. He sat at a desk all day, perhaps he didn't know how far arms and legs will stretch. Stretch in the flesh, that is, not on paper.

What oppressed, what frightened was his deception. The economic going was tough. Couldn't be helped, he said, we all would suffer. Would the Army Who Cares condemn the lives of those in its territory to an existence which was simply not acceptable? What did the distant powers who issued the orders know? We would not suffer equally. This was a war but one whose purpose had never been known, and in which no one could be sure who was the enemy, or who supported it. Yet on neither side did the Army meet resistance. On all sides, when it mattered, the word 'no' had been forgotten. They had watched it dissipate too many times recently, in too many winds.

After more than half a year, my tale ended. I did return to my home. I opened my eyes to see the red curtains which my mother had stitched with laughter. I heard familiar sounds make pleasing patterns in a bed of silence – that knock of a particular friend, the pitch of a trumpet note, warbling through the stereo speaker. Each had its own meaning, each hushed at my bidding, each was in my control.

From my tale I learned again how those deemed 'different'

are divided from those deemed 'normal', how language is distorted to disguise this division, how self is distorted, divided from its self. It made visible to me something which is pernicious, dangerous because it is invisible. It was as if I had been trapped in a bubble, with powers, procedures, professions pushing me in, keeping me in that bubble. My tale has a happy ending but we must not forget the many more tales of many more bubbles which are still waiting to be burst. My tale pales, pales, pales in comparison with reports of disabled children being forced to eat their vomit, of young people being abused, violated while 'in care'. In those reports, I recognise the perceived 'no hope' status of residents, the power of Care Staff, the power of distant bureaucrats, distant politicians, over those Care Staff, over those residents. These are the fertile breeding ground for atrocities, and even without atrocities, they cause untold harm. They thrive because we forget, if we ever knew, how to care for others, care without any capital letters or inverted commas. They thrive because all say nothing, because we think, if we think at all, there but by the grace of a god, go I.

Roz Rushworth

Mustn't Grumble

For many years I have been disabled because of arthritis. I managed to go on with my job as a sheltered housing warden for a time, but when my disability worsened and I became a wheelchair user, my life changed dramatically. I found my friends started to forsake me. One close friend – or should I say I thought she was, as we had holidayed in Europe on a number of occasions, shopped together, shared other interests, had meals at each other's homes, and so on – stopped visiting straight away. I found it so hard to come to terms with, I even wrote to her telling her how I felt, asking if I had done something wrong, without any success. Now I try to push this to the back of my mind most days. It still isn't easy as she has to pass my home to reach hers, four doors away.

At first I asked all the questions most people ask. Why me? Did I do something to make it happen? I didn't find it a help, as no answers came.

One day my youngest son visited me. I was pretty down in the dumps at the time. 'This isn't like you, Mum,' he said. 'You've never been one to brood.' I gave him a terse reply – how could he know how I felt? My life had no purpose, no one needed me, I couldn't get a job, I was useless. 'Well,' he replied, 'you made enough fuss when we were all at home' (meaning his sister and two brothers) 'because you never had time to write as you did when you were young. You have all the time in the world now and no kids to disturb you.' I thought he was completely mad, but after a few days his voice was still ringing in my ears: 'Go back to your writing.'

One night I decided I would give it a try. What had I got to lose? If I could put my hurt and frustrated feelings down on paper it might help to bring them into the open. I found it hard to begin with but, once the pen started, the ink began to flow and I couldn't stop. I sat up burning the midnight oil. My husband works at night so I didn't disturb him.

I noticed within days (yes, even my husband did too) the change in me. I was beginning to come to terms with my disability, the frustration was slowly subsiding. Where there had been anger and tears, there was laughter. When my husband struggled to dress me, fastening my bra on the wrong hook, putting my pants on back to front, I saw the funny side. I began to feel like a whole person again. Now all I had to do was get back out among people and face the world.

I called at the local library one day. I picked up a leaflet advertising a writing group; I told myself, that's for me. My husband took me along on the first night and left. There was just one young man there. He was very friendly, with a soft Irish brogue which I couldn't pick up with my hearing aid, so I smiled and nodded knowingly, not wanting him to think I was completely useless. I didn't like to tell him I am partially deaf as well.

I found I enjoyed being among people again. I had missed this contact so much. I had always dealt with the public in my working life, so I had felt very cut off.

From that group I joined VALID, a group for disabled writers. We put out our own quarterly magazine. I am still writing, setting out, editing, distributing, and so on. What a joy to be among those who accept me for myself. I am able to talk freely about my disability. No one asks why, no one expects anything of me, just to be myself, the way I am, wheelchair, warts and all. What a relief!

I joined writing workshops, finding I was able to express myself more and more with words. My horizons had widened, I no longer wallowed in self-pity, I wanted and looked forward to each new day, taking each one as it came. I made new friends and a new life, and once again enjoyed life to the full. Sometimes

I am grateful for my disability, because without it I wouldn't have this to look forward to, I would still be trying to keep up with the rat race.

I'm also a member of a drama group called Mustn't Grumble and we put on reviews. I am involved in the writing and performing. To me 'mustn't grumble' is what I say to people when I really mean 'stop asking me stupid questions' but I'm too polite to say it!

I know there are still problems for me to face, obstacles to climb over, but I have accepted myself for who I am, a person with a disability. Being able to express this in my writing has helped me so much to come to terms with it all.

All that is left now is to change the attitudes of society. To let them see that we understand our own needs. With our guidance they could get things right. We do need their support and help. I am sure if we keep on pressing this point home we will all be able to live richer and fuller lives, if only we can be given the chance to prove this.

Celeste Dandeker

Different Dances

In 1973 I was a professional dancer with the London Contemporary Dance Theatre. During a tour of Great Britain just before Christmas I fell awkwardly during a performance and broke my neck. I was just twenty-two years old. In a split second I was paralysed and faced an uncertain future. The devastation wasn't a reality to me until I sat for the first time in a wheelchair, an alien and cumbersome thing which from then on would take the place of my legs. I did not view it then as a form of mobility but as an imprisoning piece of machinery to which I was 'confined' – an end to my dance career.

Back home I found every opportunity I could to get out of it and sit on the floor away from its prominent, lofty heights where I felt embarrassed and on show. As a dancer I had felt at home as a performer in front of audiences but now I hated being in this vulnerable, disempowered position on the world's stage.

Over the following years it was important to me to keep my body in good condition, in a state of readiness, just in case! So I did exercises, albeit different ones, and have since been grateful for this discipline which was well established as a dancer.

Sixteen years after my accident, I was asked to dance in a film, *The Fall*, which was choreographed and directed by a friend, Darshan Singh Bhuller. My first response was 'Haven't you forgotten something?' But I still said yes without knowing how I was going to do it and embarked on an adventure which was the start of a whole new experience. A different dance language began to evolve, one which did not try to compete with other dancers but nevertheless emerged from the same source. Tentative, nervous explorations soon became bold gestures. I believe movement comes from within, it's not a flailing about of arms and legs. I began to be able to dance again when I understood that my body could still express feeling through movement. Although my disability is restricting, my ideas of what dance is and what dancers should look like have been challenged and liberated. My wheelchair has become another element which adds rather than detracts and sets a creative mind on fire with possibilities. It has speed and grace, a different dimension with which to choreograph.

The film appeared on television and was a success. It gave me the confidence to look for ways I could continue to dance. I was fortunate to meet people with strong spirit and vision and I now co-direct CandoCo with Adam Benjamin, a non-disabled dancer and choreographer. CandoCo is a performing contemporary dance company of eight dancers, three of whom use wheelchairs. The dancers have incredible energy, commitment and numerous skills. We teach and perform throughout the country offering a varied programme, challenging audiences and their preconceived, stereotypical views of dance and dancers. We also run dance workshops for disabled and non-disabled people who may never have had access to the joy of dance.

I feel honoured to work with the dancers in the company. I love my work and wish I had had the foresight to have started earlier.

Helen Kendall

Colostomy

Looking-through-a-crack-in-the-curtain fear, four-o'clock-in-the-morning fear, backed-into-a-corner-fear.

It was seven-thirty in the morning. I was going to have an operation for cancer of the colon at nine. I was told I would probably need a colostomy. 'Where is your normal waistline?' the colostomy care nurse asked. I put my hands around it. She marked an X a hand-width below on my left side.

Knife-edged pain, gut-deep pain, everywhere-I-look pain.

The operation lasted six hours. A senior house officer attended. She described to me what happened. 'An incision was made just below your breast bone to just below your pubic hair line and a ten-inch section of your lower bowel was removed. Your rectum was removed through an incision at your back and your anus stitched up. A small hole has been made in your stomach and that is where the colostomy is attached.'

Fingers-trapped-under-a-stone numbness, eyes-closed numbness, everyone-go-away numbness.

Nurses washed me and changed the colostomy bag. I got out of bed and walked the length of the ward. I read a magazine. I drank sips of water. I listened to the radio. I listened to the doctors discussing my condition.

Holding-on-to-a-hand love, no-questions-asked love, past-midnight love.

My sons came to visit me, glad and relieved to see me alive. They held my hands and gave me their Walkman. My friends came. They read to me. A story from the newspaper, a passage from a book. A friend washed my hair. A nurse changed my nightdress like a child in the night when I wet the bed. The doctor smiled and sat beside me.

Father-Christmas-is-not-true loss, at-home-after-the-funeral loss, never-the-same-again loss.

I attach a colostomy bag to that small opening in my stomach and replace it twice a day. I know I have no anus or rectum and part of my gut is gone. My body is strange, unusual, different.

Foul-smell-in-the-mouth anger, head-banged-against-a-wall anger, shout-out-in-the-street anger.

Why me? Was it a punishment? No one understands what I have been through, what I am suffering. I hate doctors, I hate nurses, I hate cancer, I hate the colostomy, I hate everyone and everything.

Days-away-from-home retreat, still-silent retreat, I-need-to-be-on-my-own retreat.

I sat in a garden for many days. I watched wasps leave their hole in the wall in the morning and return in the evening along the same flight-path. I listened to Bach's Suites. I watched a bee enter a flower, fill its honey sacs and move to another flower. I ate soup made from vegetables and bread hot from the toaster. I lay in the bath and looked at my scar, my hole. I looked in the mirror and introduced myself to her.

Talk-to-one-another help, say-the-word-aloud help, we-are-together help.

I visited three women in hospital who were going to have colostomies. We talked. I spoke to friends about my colostomy. I wrote about it for a newspaper. It was printed and people wrote to me and told me what had happened to them.

Eyes-wide-open hope, summer-holiday hope, yes-I-can hope.

I wrote a novel about my experiences. I worked outside my home and was scared but okay. I had returned.

Lemon-juice-on-the-tongue alive, spring-after-winter alive, Voice Alive.

I walk in the street and no one knows I have a colostomy. I choose clothes with tucks at the waist to disguise it. Like the rest of you I fart but I have no control.

Will-they-turn-away-from-me? smell, round-the-corner-in-the-playground smell, exposed smell.

The glands under my arms and in my groin swell. 'It's probably flu.' Oh yes, I expect it is, I say. I think: is it silent cancer returning in my body? I go to bed for three days and read Thomas Hardy. I feel rested, well again. I go back to my work and to my writing, changing my colostomy bag between two paragraphs.

Can-I-tread-on-the-ice uncertainty, you-all-seem-far-away uncertainty, being-alive uncertainty.

I look out of my window. Winter's over but spring not quite begun. Bulbs and birds wait for real signs of warmth.

All-the-senses-inform wisdom, no-need-to-travel-afar wisdom, here's wisdom.

Nasa Begum

Snow White

I always wanted to be an actress and when I was chosen to play the lead in my primary school play, I thought I had definitely started out on the road to fame and fortune in Hollywood. My teachers were rather short on irony, otherwise it might have occurred to them that there was something a little strange about putting on Snow White and the Seven Dwarfs in a school full of disabled children and casting me as the heroine. My classmates' approach was more direct.

– 'You're going to be painted white, Nasa Begum' they would taunt me, along with other horrendous suggestions. Yes, Snow White was without a doubt fair-skinned, and I wasn't (not to mention the other ways I didn't look like Walt Disney's version of this damsel in distress). Still, I desperately wanted the part, so I spent many anxious hours trying to convince myself that I could fit the role.

Eventually my mind was put at rest when my teacher, who was strong on kindness but weak on political awareness, told me that Snow White had dark hair like mine and in the summer was probably quite tanned from doing a lot of sunbathing. I'm not entirely sure I believed her but I wanted the part so much, I was ready to be convinced. Unfortunately, I never had the chance to make dramatic history by becoming the first Pakistani Snow White because I had to go into hospital for an operation. That's one of the stories of my life.

For one reason or another my acting career always seemed to be fated by some disaster or another. Once again seriously miscast, but enthusiastically bringing my own Islamic experience into the role of the Angel Gabriel, I tripped up and fell straight into some poor parent's lap. On another occasion I was so carried away with waving my palm around as we sang 'Hosanna' in the school Easter play (the concept of a multicultural approach to teaching hadn't yet reached my school), that I lost my balance and fell off the stage backwards. I still have a small bald patch on the top of my head to prove what dangers I was willing to undergo in the name of drama.

It was after this that I decided to redirect my enthusiasm into something that didn't seem quite so risky. I devoted most of my efforts to school work. I never liked anything to do with painting or practical things like needlework and raffia as I had already spent long spells in the hospital's Occupational Therapy department making stuffed toys, mats, bead necklaces and anything else which would encourage me to use my hands. I loved reading and writing. I don't think I was ever quite the 'girly swot' but reading was my comfort and protection. I knew that I wasn't learning as much at my school as my sisters did at theirs. They always seemed to be doing lots of interesting things and moving on at a fast pace, whereas the progress in my school was slow and repetitive.

One of the problems for me was that I spent so much time in hospital that I would miss large chunks of the school term. There was a teacher on our ward but it wasn't really equipped to cater for children who had to spend long periods of time in hospital and as I worked quickly and the resources were limited, I spent a lot of time being bored.

My 'real' school, the school that was different from the one my sisters went to, catered for children with physical disabilities from nursery school age right up until the age of sixteen. We were all transported to and from school in single decker buses as children came there from all over the city. For some of us, by the time we arrived at school we had already been travelling for over an hour. The bus journey was one of the best parts of the school day because the activities we had started in the playground would extend into the journey to and from school. You could make or break friends, play games and share gossip. I used to enjoy waiting on the pavement each morning, there seemed to be something special about being collected for school from my own doorstep. I used to chat to the milkman, the postman and the families on their way to the primary school which was right next door.

It was not a very big school but there was an enormous range of ability levels within each class. There were children who never seemed to be able to finish their work whilst others would be impatiently looking around for something else to do. I think I was somewhere in between. I could do the work without much difficulty but I was very slow in getting it down on paper. It wasn't until I went away to boarding school that anyone acknowledged that my lack of writing skills was due to my physical condition rather than to an inability to study.

I didn't do as much academic work as my sisters in mainstream schools, and one of the reasons for this was the bane of my life – physiotherapy. I was sure that I was being treated unjustly as not everyone in my class had to go away to these sessions and, what was worse, it didn't even exist at my sisters' school. I couldn't see the point of all these agonising exercises. I was never very good at accepting the fact that things I didn't like could be 'good for me' and the physiotherapist managed to do a really good job of making me a conscientious objector for the rest of my life. I was certain that there were not many physiotherapists who would allow someone to pull their limbs in agonising directions on the unlikely grounds that it would 'make them better'.

It never occurred to me to question the fact that this was the sort of school I should go to, or to ask to go to school with my sisters. I knew that I was different but it wasn't something that was an issue for me. On the whole I used to enjoy school a lot and looked forward to Mondays and the end of the holidays. As a little girl I would ask the teachers to give me homework and eagerly present it to them the next morning. I became less keen on working after school when people told me I had to do it.

The kids at my school were like kids in any other school. There were the hard kids in the gang who would rant and rave and there were the wet blankets who nobody wanted to know.

I was in the middle. Unlike many girls, I never sought the devotion of one best friend and was happy to wander round making friends with whoever crossed my path.

As a child it was hard for me to accept that there were two distinct ways I was different from the majority, not like the people I saw on the TV, in the comics and books I read. At school everyone had some form of disability so no one was picked on just for that. But disabled kids are just like everyone else and they would tease out and pick on anyone who was different. I had never thought about it before I started school but I soon learnt what it meant to be black in a predominantly white establishment. I used to get very upset at the relentless name-calling, 'blackie' 'nigger' 'paki', but grassing on anyone was not on so I had to learn to live with it.

It was hard, though, and it made me feel out of place wherever I was. My mum used to sew me the Salwar Kamiz, matching silk dresses and trousers, like she did for my sisters, but they just attracted further derogatory remarks at school until I begged her to let me stop wearing them. Eventually she relented and bought me Western-style trousers and dresses. Even this didn't help because my culture said that girls should wear both trousers and dresses but according to my school friends this was the pits of fashion. I ended up feeling uncomfortable in the clothes I wore at school and at home and I tried to solve this dilemma by wearing Western clothes at school and changing immediately I returned. For almost fifteen years I did not allow white people to see me in Salwar Kamiz.

There was only one other Asian girl at my school and I always admired her. It was worship from afar. She was in the Seniors and I was just a Junior but I saw her on the school bus each day. She had a wonderful dress sense and beautiful long black hair which fell from her shoulders right down to the base of her spine. I was desperate for long hair but as I wore a brace from my neck downwards it was almost impossible to let it grow. Everything about this girl fascinated me, not least the fact that her family owned a shop which seemed like a palace to me, full of Asian and Western clothes.

Then came the tragedy of the Orange Dress. I was about nine at the time, orange was my favourite colour and I was in love with that dress. Every day when the school bus stopped for her to get in, I would see it in the window of her family's shop. I wanted it so much. Eventually I managed to persuade my mum to let me have it for the school party and she gave the money to the bus lady to buy it when we stopped at the shop to drop the girl off on the way home. The dress was there in the morning but by the time we came home, it was gone! My heart was broken. My beloved dress had been sold and there were no more in my size. There was no consoling me and it took a couple of years for me to live down the 'story of the orange dress'. I think what upset me most was that I wanted that dress and I wanted it from that shop. Most of all I wanted the girl whose family owned that dress shop to be my friend.

She was the only black role model I had. Her culture was very different from mine and her experience of family life was not the same, but the fact that she was at my school was important for me. Until I met her, I had never seen another Asian person with a disability and I was proud to be considered to be like her.

But it was still quite a shock for me to realise that the other kids at school saw us as being quite different from them. I don't remember race being an issue in the hospital where I spent a lot of my childhood and there were so many Asian people where I lived that I did not stand out as being black. It took me a long time to understand why people who did not know me in my neighbourhood called me 'spastic', 'bandy legs' or 'Ironside' and why people with disabilities called me 'paki' or 'nigger'. Eventually I learned that wherever I went I would probably stand out as being different from the majority and I had to be prepared to accept being called either paki or bandy legs, and sometimes both.

At least at primary school I developed an awareness of being black through the very blatant approach adopted by my schoolmates. It is easier to cope with the uninhibited forms of discrimination used by children than the subtle approach adopted by adults. Children are usually willing to be given explanations and to learn about what it means to be black or disabled and why discrimination is wrong. Adults find it much harder to recognise their own prejudices, they use their own misconceptions to convince themselves that they are right.

Looking back, I find it hard to believe that I was denied the right to have the same education as my sisters, that they went to the primary school right next to our house, whilst I travelled for an hour across town. At playtime my mum used to pass them fruit through the fencing that divided our garden from the school playground. But I've come a long way since the days of Snow White and orange dresses. I've reclaimed my identity by refusing to accept a concept of 'normality' which tells me I must walk, have fair skin and try to blend in by wearing Western clothes.

Caroline Ball

Shopping

Shopping alone was a long time ago
with a bicycle basket on the side of my chair;
down the tarmac drive and over the dyke,
across the bridge with no sides
where Mum used to worry sky-high,
but Dad would say
'Let her go and see if she comes back.'

Outside the supermarket
butterflies funny in my stomach,
I squeezed the hooter on my chair,
the black hooter to call the man
to read the list in my purse
to bring the goods from the shop shelves,
where I could not go.

Shopping in the basket,
butterflies now flown,
electric as my chair
I whizzed along the quiet lane
home:
to Mum – anxious with barriers of love,
to Dad – loving by letting me go
to grow up,
to try it alone.

Jennifer Hoskins

For Those Not Yet Angry

Okay, I want to set up
a little scenario here,
can you for a moment
just imagine that you

are walking happily along a
path (and, yes, I know walking
is hard for some – but if
it is you'll find this whole

exercise easier) when around a
corner you espy a set
of steps and there are say,
eight of them and as this

dawns (your thinking hasn't been
too good lately) you realise
that you haven't the strength
to climb these steps and instead

you have to turn back or maybe
sit down and rest somewhere
(but there isn't a bench) or maybe
you could go very slowly and

take half an hour over them
and someone will ask you

(sarcastically) if you're waiting
for a bus. Yes, I know you've

been here before and you're
accustomed to seeing giant
obstacles where other people barely
notice concrete steps but this

time before you turn back I want
you to pause and consider
and to become perfectly
clear in your own mind that

you don't deserve this and to
ask yourself how you actually
feel about it and how I
want you to feel is furious.

Lois Keith

Anger – Early Days

(A School Association meeting at my children's school to discuss
putting in a safer ramp)

Next time I will get angry.
I will hear my own voice loud and clear
It will not tremble and fold in on itself
Never again.
Not ever will I expose myself
To your calm, white, mild-mannered complacency
To your 'couldn't we look at it another way'
Your 'I'm sorry if I put it the wrong way but what
   I mean is'
Your 'I think that the constitution actually says'
Your 'could you tell me what the Authority's position
   on this issue is'
And when my voice refused not to shake
And I let you see my half face falling to pieces
   as I wheeled out the room
With the sound of my weeping echoing to you from down
   the corridor,
Why then, then you must have felt grey bad enough to say
– 'I think there must have been one or two
   misunderstandings'
– 'Lois didn't seem to realise that'

But in the room not one of you
Could break your soft-centred, well-reasoned mould
No not one.

In discomfort you moved your chairs
Your body language removed you from the circle.
You spoke in measured terms of organisation,
Of protocol, of policy
But mostly you spoke of silence.

And not one of you, not one
Was prepared to break the feeling of that meeting
And speak in clear support.
You thought it was unfair that I should embarrass you
By showing what I felt.

And afterwards in the pub you said to each other
'It's a shame Lois was so emotional about it,
Doesn't she realise we all have her interests at heart?'
You don't.
You wouldn't realise a clear, strong, committed statement
If one got up and hit you in the face
And that's what I should have wanted to do to you.

Eeny meeny miney mo
Catch a cripple by her toe
If she hollers ...
Next time I still may not know how to holler
So there won't be a next time.
Not with you.
Never.
I will wait until my new shell grows
And while it does I will protect myself
From your pious, ever-so-well-meaning, calm destruction.

Lois Keith

Tomorrow I'm Going to Rewrite the English Language

Tomorrow I am going to rewrite the English Language.
I will discard all those striving ambulist metaphors
of power and success
And construct new ways to describe my strength.
My new, different strength.

Then I won't have to feel dependent
Because I can't stand on my own two feet.
And I'll refuse to feel a failure
When I don't stay one step ahead.
I won't feel inadequate if I can't
Stand up for myself
Or illogical when I don't
Take it one step at a time.

I will make them understand that it is a very male way
To describe the world.
All this walking tall
And making great strides.

Yes, tomorrow I am going to rewrite the English Language
Creating the world in my own image.
Mine will be a gentler, more womanly way
To describe my progress.
I will wheel, cover and encircle.
Somehow I will learn to say it all.

PART TWO

Molly Holden

'Along the lane . . .'

Along the lane go two of almost
   equal height, her arm
through his. She takes my place, so sweet
   a surrogate no harm

enters my mind. Yet I can hardly bear
   to watch my daughter
on her father's arm. Salt in the wound.
   Fate gives no quarter.

Lois Keith

This Week I've Been Rushed Off My Wheels

Some weeks come together and some are full of separate days. This is a seven stories week.

On Monday I had a puncture. Amazingly the first in nearly eight years. Monday and Tuesday are my school days. I teach English in a big comprehensive in the middle of London. 10P were listening, unusually rapt, as I read Rosa Guy's novel *The Friends*.

'Oh look, Miss,' said Akbar suddenly, holding a drawing pin in the air, 'I've just pulled this out of your tyre, shall I put it back again?' (He did. Two punctures instead of one.) He held it for me to see. We all looked up. 'Oh, Miss', said Mitchell, 'I can hear your tyre going down.' He made the noise through his teeth – *sssss*.

'Don't be silly,' I said, and we read on as beautiful Ramona rips her dress down to the waist to reveal to her shocked children and husband the scars where her breast had been. 'Calvin,' she says, 'they must take this lesson from us. This lesson of how life twists us so that we put value on worthless things. Puts beauty before you to blind you to what beauty really is.' The class were stunned (it's not often they get naked bodies on a Monday morning), while I wondered if pushing like that was possible, imagining myself in a heap in the corridor in front of all the kids. My tyres and I both sighed. Ahh.

In the office I was definitely shaky. My colleagues were surprised and made me cups of tea. Inside I felt stranded like a frail raft at sea.

At lunchtime I sat in my car whilst Peter from the Physics Department mended my tyre with his puncture kit. Ellie, Head of Special Needs, was keen to have a go. 'That's brilliant,' she said. 'I've always wanted to know how to do this. It'll be really useful when I do the London to Brighton Friends of the Earth Bike Ride this Saturday.'

I rang Colin. He worried and came home early with a bunch of flowers. I rang Jenny. She laughed and said 'God, how awful,' and told me how that morning her lift had broken and how she'd had to bump herself down forty-three steps to make the breakfast.

I went to bed early remembering how it had felt wheeling through the empty corridors leaning to the left, insecure and unbalanced. I hadn't fallen. I hadn't made a fool of myself. Everything was all right. I fell asleep thinking how fragile it is, my grasp of independence.

On Tuesday I forgot all about it. 10P and I read more of *The Friends* and learned from Rosa Guy how hard it is to be a young, black fifteen-year-old girl growing up in Harlem and how bad it feels to betray your best friend. At half past four I left school, my teaching days done – until Sunday when I would spend the evening marking and preparing.

At six o'clock I hit the road again. I was in an optimistic mood. Nervous though. I'm always nervous about going somewhere new. This anxiety is rarely a social one, it isn't about meeting new people or feeling shy. I had thirty-five standing up years to deal with that one. This 'normal' anxiety is displaced for me by the sheer physical concern of going to a place I haven't been before. Of finding a place to park, worrying about whether I can get out of the car straight on to the pavement, whether there will be kerbs. It's anxiety about asking a total stranger (if there is a total stranger to ask) to help me in some way. It's the fear that there will be some obstacle no one has told me about – a step, a bollard, a pothole, a locked door.

But tonight I felt sure it would be okay. The guy on the phone had sounded so knowing and helpful. I'd told him exactly what I needed, I'd made it crystal clear. He said he'd sort it out, someone would be there to help, he'd be at the meeting himself. He hadn't called me back as he said he would, but was it likely that a theatre company for disabled people would organise a workshop for disabled writers in a place inaccessible for wheelchair users? Of course not.

I'd left home early. The map they'd sent me was unreadable but I'd written down the address when I'd spoken to him on the phone. Interchange Studios, Wilkin Street. I found it, although it certainly wasn't easy. A gloomy, between the railway lines sort of place. Glum housing estates, poor lighting, cul de sacs, no man's land. Certainly no woman's land, I thought, seeing a solitary female wandering down the dark alley, searching like me, I learned later, for our workshop.

I had driven down a long, narrow drive signposted Interchange Studios. At the end there was no parking, no visible entrance, no way to get in. I telephoned from the car (lucky me to have such equipment). No answer. I sat in the dark for five minutes willing someone to appear and show me how to get in. It was then I saw it, a little sign just inside my vision. Entrance to Interchange Studios has now moved to Danby Street. Where the hell was Danby Street?

It was now six-twenty. I looked it up in the *A to Z*. This area had more roads per square inch than any other part of London. I reversed all the way up the lane, my idea of a nightmare, back to the main road. No right turn, dead ends, three point turns, reversing round corners, until I finally found, emblazoned in lights: Interchange Studios.

Completely inaccessible. A dark, rainy night, nowhere to park, no way to get in. Huge bollards, an unbelievably steep and cambered concrete slope, chicken wire fence and no one there. I telephoned again. From the car I could see lights on, lots of people in the building. No reply. 'Don't cry,' I said to myself firmly. 'Don't cry, you're not to cry.' It never works.

By this time I was late and I was angry. Then two young

women passed, black jeans and long hair, carrying musical instruments. 'Excuse me,' I called out. I didn't want to have this conversation. To talk to strangers you have to be pleasant and jolly and that wasn't how I felt. They stopped, looked at me, looked suspicious. I didn't want to have to say this. 'I'm disabled, I use a wheelchair and I can't get into the building. I wonder if you would mind seeing if there's someone from the writing workshop in there and ask them to come out and see me.' Out came the man from reception, bearded, smiling, not unfriendly. I asked him to find someone from this workshop to talk to me. I was wound up like a top. I just wanted to say my piece and go. I wanted to be at home.

'This is what the *world* does to us,' I said to the young woman who appeared. 'We shouldn't do this to each other. How dare they organise something for disabled people in a venue like this and not tell anyone about it? How dare they think that's okay? There's no one here to meet me, no one answers the phone. I've let other people down to even come here. I should have been somewhere else but I wanted to come. I ring up, I ask all the right questions. I get here and I can't get in the fucking building.' And then I cried.

Unusually, she listened and wasn't defensive. She didn't tell me that I was over-reacting or that it wasn't her fault. She said, 'It's awful, it's awful. Can I give you a hug?'

'No you can't.' This was my rage and I didn't want to share it.

'No one told me. Why didn't they give you my phone number? It shouldn't have happened. I'm so sorry, I've had a bloody awful day myself.' And then she burst into tears and we were both crying.

'Oh God,' I thought, dismayed at her tears, pleased she wasn't accusing me. 'Come on,' I said crying, laughing, supporting her now, 'I might as well go in, I've come this far.'

So together we negotiated the awful ramp, backwards so I didn't fall out, whilst she explained to me that this was temporary and soon there would be a proper car-park with proper spaces for disabled drivers. We went through endless corridors with chipboard room dividers and sinks with noticeboards, until we reached the room where eight people were sitting round a table with their eyes closed and a woman with a round face and brown wavy hair was saying softly, 'I want you to imagine you have something in your hands – some very special possession which only you have. I want you to think about its shape, its special smell, its feelings, and when you have it all clear in your mind I want you to write it down.

So I wrote:

> My anger has no shape.
> It's fierce, it hurts,
> it's futile.
> I want to aim it at the person sitting at this table
> who deserves it.
> Let him eat it,
> let him keep its bitterness.

After that I began to feel better and when it came to my turn I read it out. 'Mmm,' said our workshop leader, 'thank you,' and with her mouth slightly twisted, moved quickly on.

Wednesday was a day for me.

In the morning Rachel and Miriam got themselves ready for school and, sensing somehow that I was not entirely with them, made me tea 'in the cup or in the pot?' and a crumpet with jam. Not that we don't fight, we do. But not this morning, for which I was very grateful. Our fights are the sort of fights that all strong mothers have with strong daughters, I think. I get more than averagely irritable with them when they leave their things on the floor so that I can't get around and I'm not always good enough at hiding my raw feelings from them. I don't want them to feel they have to worry about me.

People used to say that they were like a little one and a big one of the same thing but now they are growing to be very different. Rachel is eleven, tall and slim and, as her grandfather put it, getting a shape. She is loving and thoughtful, funny and complicated, and is going through a difficult phase which looks like it's going to last until she's at least thirty. Miriam, who is nearly nine, is rounder, sunny natured and affectionate. She is learning to be difficult but it doesn't come easily to her. She adores her big sister who loves her back, even when they fight, which is mercifully rare.

Rachel was three and Miriam just two weeks past her first birthday when I was run over by a speeding driver in Australia. My separation from them, my inability to be their mother, was more painful than knowing I would never walk again. People who do not live with a disability find this impossible to understand. Now I try to be a strong enough mother to them, and mostly I succeed. They understand more than other children about fairness and justice and why disabled people have to be fighters. They don't like the way people stare at us when we're out together and have an acute awareness of when people are being patronising. When someone passes the three of us going about our business in the supermarket or the shopping centre and smiles in a sickening way muttering 'How sweet', or asks me (or them) if I'd mind telling them how I came to be in a wheelchair, we imagine replying, 'It's a disease that strikes people who say stupid things.' We don't, of course.

I like being out with my children and I know that it's not just because I like their company, which is a good reason, but because it normalises me in the eyes of the public, which is not. They're still not too old to want to climb on my lap and have 'taxi rides' to bed. I don't want them to grow up too quickly. It will be hard to let them go.

It is bliss to have a whole day to work, muse and reflect, until three-thirty that is. I want it both ways. Within the loving cocoon of my family, I need time to be by myself. When I first started writing after my accident it was to save myself from the kind of despair I didn't know was possible. One of the first things I wrote about was the idea that I would never be alone again, that I would never be able to wander about or sit in a cafe eating something delicious, reading a book with no one knowing where I was. A year or two later when I rediscovered the trick of being alone, it felt wonderful.

So today, after I took the children to school, I came home, made myself a pot of good coffee and took it into the Room Of My Own. Well nearly. It does have the computer in it which the entire family wants to share, but it is still called 'Mummy's Room'. I was more fortunate than many; the courts ruled that my paraplegia was someone else's fault and I received compensation. Together Colin and I built a beautiful, light house in the middle of London and in it I have this funny triangular wedge, which Rachel called the 'Brie Shaped Room' when she first saw it. It has a wooden floor and a beige and blue Persian rug which belonged to my brother. I have what Alice Walker describes as a most desirable feature in a working room, a view of the garden, and it is full of bright pictures and postcards. Today is a day for me.

On Thursday I went for lunch with my friend Sally. We met after my accident. Sometimes I classify things like that, before or after. Increasingly these days it doesn't seem important.

I met Sally at playgroup. I found it hard in those early days to socialise with all the mums each morning and one day I rather guiltily asked three-year-old Miriam if she'd made any friends. She said she had a friend called Thomas. Later I learned that of the twenty-four children in Highbury Playgroup, four were called Thomas, so it was quite possible I'd cornered the wrong mum. Still, it didn't matter because Sally and I liked each other.

Sally thinks I'm AMAZING. This gets in the way of our friendship because although sometimes I am amazing, I am never AMAZING. When we're out together I make her nervous. I don't want to but I do. Negotiating the kerbs of busy Upper Street on another wet afternoon, she hovered over me, unable to accept that I would tell her when I needed help. It reminded me rather of learning how to quickstep at the Arthur Murray School of Dancing with my brother when I was eleven. We both wanted to make the moves, and we were getting in each other's way. Still, Sally is my friend and she's clever and funny so I try not to let it matter.

After our meal I was getting into my car when the all-too-familiar happened. In a busy road, with cars parked on both sides, I kept the traffic waiting whilst I folded my wheelchair into the nifty mechanical hoist which stacks it on the roof of my car. A thirty-something, City banker, BMW type approached, offering much-unneeded help, and tried to close the door, which clearly wouldn't shut what with the hoist very slowly moving its way up.

I was pleased with the way I dealt with this one, uttering a pithy phrase like 'Leave my door alone, you stupid idiot, can't you see you'll just have to wait' and at the exact moment, slamming the door shut. Furious, his face now scarlet, he swore at me through the closed window, insisting he was only trying to be helpful.

What can you expect? I turned to Sally, expecting solidarity, sympathy. Hadn't I for once been AMAZING, dealing so adeptly with one of the pillocks of this world? Silence. Sally did not approve. She was upset and thought I had been unfair. She wasn't proud of me.

We began to talk about the unspoken layers of difference between us. Her dislike of aggression, my feeling that it is sometimes the only way I can deal with the world. Her feeling that in rejecting genuine help, I was rejecting her. My feeling that she had to accept my definition and understanding of the world. I lived it. I knew how thinly people disguised their patronage, fear and dislike of people who were different, people who were disabled. Her feeling that there was more rage here than she could deal with. We both cried. We made up. I respect her for wanting to talk about it honestly, but it hurt us both.

Later there was Colin to tell it all to. We may disagree and argue about everything, from who said they'd buy the butter on the way home from work to who does the most loving and supporting in this relationship, but on this we never disagree. My definition of the world as a disabled person has become his. If I come home from work telling him how everyone stood in the lift looking at me and none of my colleagues would move so that I was five minutes late for my lesson, he never asks me to look at it from their point of view. My anger is his anger. Miraculously, I am the same person for him as he is for me.

On Friday. The Weekend Starts Here, as they used to say on *Ready Steady Go*, but this Friday, I have to say, was a killer. The day was fine. I prepared for the Women's Day on Saturday, took the children to their dance class, made supper for them and the babysitter, and then we went to the cinema. I'd rung up, booked the tickets, told them I needed an aisle seat, told them why. This cinema, arty and modern, has lots of stairs but great films. Colin's good at this type of thing, we lived for a year in a house with three floors.

Outside it was raining – it's been raining all week. Inside it was packed with the kind of audience who respond to good reviews in the *Guardian* and *Time Out*. We collected our tickets from the box office and, moving through the crowd, Colin began to bump me down the long flight of stairs, like Christopher Robin with Winnie the Pooh only forwards. Near the top we were stopped by a man with a black pony-tail and the sleeves of his jacket rolled up so you could see the silk lining. The conversation went something like this:

Him: Are you going downstairs?
Us: Yes.
Him: (*To Colin*) Can she get out and walk?
Us: No.
Him: Well you can't take that wheelchair downstairs. It's against the Fire Regulations.
Colin: (*It's hard for me to talk at an angle of forty-five degrees – bump, bump, bump.*) We've bought our tickets and we've been here several times before.
Him: Well, they shouldn't have sold them to you, I can't let you in.
Colin: This is ridiculous, it's fascism. It's like telling someone they can't come in because they're black.

By this time we were halfway down, turning the corner to the second flight. Managers in trendy cinemas in Camden get very edgy when you mention racism. They don't think of disability like that.

Him: It's not my fault. I don't make the rules. I'm sorry but I can't let you in, it's not safe, there might be a fire.

Colin: Do you ask everyone for a Health Certificate before you let them in, then? No entry if you've had a triple bypass? I can carry my wife out in two minutes.

By this time we were at the bottom of the stairs. Finally I could speak, on the level.

I'm going to get into my seat and watch this film. You can call the police if you want to but they'll have to physically remove me and I'll scream.

I don't know where these words came from, I surprised myself. It was as if I'd had them sitting in my head all this time waiting for the right moment.

The film told the story of a poor Indian girl wrenched from her mother into a life of prostitution. I cried for us both. Still, between me and unbearable sadness is a box of Terry's Neapolitan chocolates. I ate the lot.

After the film the nice usher told us he was very sorry about what had happened and that it would be better to come on an afternoon in the week than an evening at the weekend. This, of course, ignores the fact that I look after my children and go out to work, and so does the person who gets me into inaccessible cinemas. It's also hard to understand how you can be a health and safety hazard on a Friday night but not on a Tuesday afternoon, or why you're not allowed in a cinema with stairs in Camden but you're all right half a mile away in Westminster. Anyway, they won. I'll never go back.

Afterwards we went as arranged to have a drink with some friends who hadn't been able to get a babysitter. We'd all been to this cinema a month or two before. They were shocked by what we told them, shocked at my distress.

They listened and tried to see themselves in my place. You go to a movie and you have tickets but they say you can't come in. They try to throw you out and they have the law on their side. We all had another drink.

Saturday was the Annual Women's Day held at the Spinal Injuries Unit at Stanmore. Twenty-one of us, women of all ages, from all backgrounds, all four feet high, came together as we have done for five years, some straight from the wards. Joanna, Lynn and I have organised this every year with help from the staff at the hospital.

It felt good to be there. Old friends tried rather unsuccessfully to hug, wheelchairs clashing. New people met more shyly. All day we talked, ate, painted plates, listened to speakers, had make-up put on, looked at books. We laughed about the kind of things we talk about together, recognising that although we may not have met before, none of us are strangers.

Indwelling, intermittent, firing off, evacuation, pressure marks, attitude, access is our shared vocabulary. But so is men, women, love, sex, children, friends, houses, food, music and work.

I went home tired. It had been a good day.

On Sunday I stayed at home. Colin and I read the papers, relaxed and didn't get up till late. Rachel tore herself away from the television after only a few hints and brought us tea in bed. The children came in for hugs and wanted to play 'The Game of Life'. We refused and stayed in bed some more.

Getting ready for the day was the difficult part. It always seems like hard work and somehow today, with all that time in front of me, it seemed even harder. *1* Transfer out of bed. *2* Transfer from wheelchair to shower seat. *3* Have shower and wash hair. And so on. Back on the bed I roll from side to side putting on knickers, then tights, then skirt, then shoes. On extreme days I give myself a number of rolls to aim for.

These days I dress in a kind of uniform which suits my needs. Black or navy fine wool skirt, sometimes patterned. Black or navy opaque tights. Dark polo-neck cotton top or shirt. Sometimes a bit of colour in a jumper or a scarf. Often a necklace, always earrings. Turning forty-three this year, I bought myself my first lip brush and some bright red lipstick. I'm not sure what this means exactly.

If I had one wish it would be to make a spell each morning and appear fully washed and dressed in my wheelchair. I never wish that I could walk again. That's not to say it doesn't hurt sometimes. Usually it's things that are out of the ordinary of my daily life, like a friend recounting the wonderful holiday he's just spent trekking in the Peak District with his family or watching my children with their father exploring the Tomb of the Kings whilst I sit looking down at them. But to wish that I could walk again would be wanting to turn myself into something so completely different that I wouldn't know who I was any more. Like wishing I was a man or wishing I was Japanese.

My wishes are smaller, and increasingly these days to do with vanity, like wishing I had thick curly hair. Or wishing that I was thinner, something which should be in my control but never is, quite. Or wishing that I could wear narrow beige linen dresses. But really I am who I am and these days, that's the person I'm comfortable with.

This Sunday I didn't much fancy cooking and as a treat for lunch we ate smoked salmon beigels with cream cheese and New Green cucumbers. In the afternoon, I got on my scooter and went for a ride to Highbury Fields with the children on their bikes. Colin stayed at home and listened to 'his music' which none of us can stand.

By the evening, I had abandoned any idea that I might work and tried not to think about the consequences for tomorrow. I lay on the sofa and watched television instead. All week I had been at odds with life and now I still felt unsettled.

But that night I slept like a baby.

Anna Sullivan

Summer Poetry

Summer poetry is what you called my writing.
Funny, I never thought of it like that.
So was all the grief and pain of my
Winter poetry just a seasonal emotion?
Is what I write now just full of sun
And azure skies to sleep under?
I think you may find a few shadows
Lurking around the patio.
But then you didn't really mean that, did you?

Once a month we meet now instead of every day,
And you smile and give me herbal tea
To drink and say how well I look and I smile
Back, then we talk about music and
My diet and share a joke then we
Both look at our diaries and I leave.

But I have so many more things
To say to you, that I cannot, because
You have absorbed my grief for so long
Now, that to give you more would show
In your eyes every time that you
Look at me, so it lies hidden in my
Summer poetry skulking beneath
The deckchairs and shimmering heat.

Janice Pink

What Happened To You?

Well, that's what people ask you. Then they ask if it was an accident, sniffing for BLOOD. Sometimes I tell them I got hit by a meteorite. So then they recommend some cure-all programme that would have done so much for Fred-up-the-road if he hadn't died first. Or an incredibly expensive 'alternative' potion – winkles' gonads, rhinoceros spit, eye of newt and toe of frog.

When I was eleven, my back ached and my knees hurt.

'Growing pains!' said the doctor. 'Exercise is what she needs!'

Father bought me a bike, and taught me to ride it, in fifty terrifying lessons. Father was prone to panic in situations that would have been fine if he hadn't made them so stressful. And there was nothing wrong with *his* offspring. How dare they? The very thought!

He'd cycle beside me as I wobbled down a steep hill, and suddenly yell 'Look out!'

I'd glimpse the towering red cliff of a London bus, then crash into the kerb and fall painfully. Father said I only needed CONFIDENCE. Cycling made me puff till my chest hurt and I groaned for breath.

'Out of condition!' said Father, and made me ride round the block again.

'Overweight!' said the doctor, and gave me a diet sheet of gourmet nibbles for rabbits.

I pedalled for nerve-racking miles, I did knee-bends and touch-toes, I ate acres of lettuce. My back hurt, I wheezed, and I grew and grew.

When I was sixteen, nearly six feet tall, and still in pain, I went to another doctor.

'Well, well,' he said. 'Can't be much wrong with a buxom wench like you!'

Obviously, if you're disabled, you should look fragile, which I didn't then and never will now.

When I was twenty-eight and expecting my third child, I skidded down the stairs on my back. After months of pain, and aeons of Outpatients, a doctor finally diagnosed 'a touch of arthritis'. Touch of a sledgehammer. Nobody believed me, they all told me I was too young to have arthritis, which was then thought to be for elderly people, like cut-price perms.

Doctors came and went, so did the pain. When I was thirty-four, I had my first serious attack of asthma. I've had many more spectacular ones since – clanging ambulance jobs, chest ward, the works. But that one was scary enough.

Soon after, my back gave out temporarily, and I spent a whole week in bed, while my husband beat his breast and called aloud to the Heavens, asking what he had done to deserve a sick wife. I had another bout of asthma, and another doctor said it was psychosomatic, and that he didn't believe in inhalers anyway.

And so it went on, and the years passed, and thorns grew up around the castle gates, and my handsome prince was getting to be more of a pain in the arse than the arthritis. And when the castle was in need of rewiring, and bits of drainpipe were hanging off the walls, the handsome prince lost all his money on the Derby, said 'Illness is all in your mind,' and got a bit too free with his fists.

So I divorced him, and he said I always made a bloody fuss about nothing anyway.

Which left me in a mid-life crisis with three children, a chronically ill parent to care for, loads of debts, dangling drainpipes and the menopause. I also had a dog and three cats, pretty sparks round the light bulbs and a crush on the Vicar's wife. Did I even mention arthritis and asthma? Of course not. No one else did.

I went to work. Part-time in a bookshop, part-time as a Home Help, and practically full-time making celebration cakes at exorbitant prices, so my kids could have school blazers like everyone else. I coped with teenagers stamping up and down stairs being misunderstood, paid the bills, got the house repaired by a cowboy with a Mercedes, had hot flushes and thought I should get the dog spayed.

I fought to get walking and bathroom aids for mother, and pushed her out in her wheelchair on Saturdays. I got an injunction to stop my ex living in an insanitary motor caravan right outside the house, and found myself a therapist. When my back hurt from head to heels I baked it on an electric blanket and swallowed painkillers.

After four years of this, my lowest discs finally eroded with a red-hot crunch of collapsing vertebrae, and the Local Authority 'retired' me from the Home Help Service. The bookshop closed, the ex went to Clacton and the dog had seven pups. I told the therapist I thought I was a lesbian and she took it quite well.

I still never thought of myself as disabled – well, I was looking after mother, who needed more and more help, though I had managed to organise a District Nurse, the Travelling Library Service and a Day Centre for her. I tried for a Home Help, but Social Services said it wasn't necessary as Mother had me. Still, I was happy. My most precious possessions were a Ventolin Inhaler and a Decree Absolute – I could cope.

I always said I wasn't going to make a career out of being disabled. If I was, I mean. The doctors took about thirty years to realise I had a disability or two, and it took me a further ten to accept it. As they say – I didn't *look* disabled . . .

However, now I'm OFFICIAL. I have a Disabled Parking space outside the house, I collect all the appropriate benefits, and Social Services have put extra little legs on my armchair. I use a noticeable walking aid, and puff at my inhaler as my joints creak grindingly. I am a real, gen-u-ine, card carrying Registered Disabled Person.

THAT's what happened to me.

Suna Polio

Being Sam's Mum

Sam hands us daffodils in the rediscovered March garden, and puts his near his lips and blows, like you'd blow a windmill. So the three of us stand there seriously blowing our daffodil windmills.

Sam rushes out of the house with his hat and coat and ball, off out for the morning with friends, rushing to meet life with never a backward glance at his two mummies smiling and waving goodbye.

Sam lies on top of me grinding his forehead all over my face in an act that says unmistakably, I love you to bits. Sam jumps right into the middle of the puddle, Sam runs naked across the living room, arms out behind him, calling 'Wheeeeeeee!', Sam nuzzles his head into the warm nook where my neck and shoulder meet, and falls asleep.

This Sam is my son.

But what's this about his two mummies? I mean, come on, we all know that children only have one mummy. One mummy and, if they're lucky, one daddy. Two mummies, frankly, is a bit excessive, not natural, and hang on a minute, does that mean that you're, you know, lesbians?

And which one of you is the *real* mum?

If you saw me and Ann and Sam together, what would you decide about us? What story would you tell yourself to make sense of the picture we make? Of course, one of us must be his mum, that's obvious. Who would you choose? Perhaps you'd wait and see who picked him up and perched him on her hip, who buckled him into his buggy and strode off to the shops with him. Or perhaps you'd wait for that biggest of all giveaways, who changed his nappy.

She who swoops and grabs, she who totes, she who is in physical possession, is the mother. This is the public image of motherhood, so much part of our culture that it's never spoken of, never challenged.

If these are the signs you'd be looking for to help you decide who the real mother is, you wouldn't choose me. I'm disabled. I don't go to the shops with Sam on my own, we've always needed a third party; my swooping and grabbing has been strictly limited and I haven't changed his nappy since he decided that it was good fun to be chased round the room by a red-faced somebody waving a fresh nappy at him and shouting 'Come back, come back'.

When Sam was a baby sometimes we'd walk around a shopping precinct or down the high street with him sitting on my lap whilst Ann pushed me in my wheelchair. For the odd half-hour I would occupy that public space, be that public image, woman in possession of baby. It was my lap he sat on, my chest he leaned into, my warmth mingling with his. Surely to the world we must now look like mother and child?

Not so. While I was rejoicing in the freedom of movement, the bustle of the precinct and the visibility of my relationship with Sam, I was being judged powerless and incapable by people on the streets. Why? Their perception of the wheelchair of course. If I'd been with a man, the picture we made may have been interpreted differently. As it was, we were two women and a baby. To the public eye I looked an unlikely candidate for motherhood. The wheelchair disqualified me.

The woman who works in the greengrocer's made this clear to me when I went into her shop after I'd been out with Ann and Sam. 'I saw your friend taking you out with her baby the other day,' she chirped.

This is the lot of the disabled lesbian mother, for we are often out with our children and another woman. It's called being a family.

There is another way of making your relationship to a young one clear. A way that doesn't involve hefting and toting. It's to claim it in words. To say 'I'm his mother'. Simple, eh? Well, actually, no, it's not simple at all. Perhaps it would be easier if Sam had grown inside me, come out of me, if my biology was all tangled up with his. Yes, of course that would make it easier to make the possessive claim out loud. Do with words what my body doesn't demonstrate. But he didn't. And this small fact opens up a chasm of doubt, misunderstanding, fear, complexity.

My attempts to talk about my son to a few trusted people outside my immediate sphere have been laden with awkwardness and embarrassment and for a long time I gave it up as a bad job.

In the early weeks after Sam's birth it was different. Sometimes pride, and the desire to let people I work with know about this momentous thing that was happening in my life, tempted me to start talking about him. We would soon trip over ourselves. The conversation would go something like this:

'What you been up to lately, Sue?'

'We've just had a baby.'

Confusion – they haven't seen me pregnant.

'How are you feeling?'

'A bit tired, but it's great.'

'Oh – other disabled women I know have been laid up for ages when they've had a baby.'

And here we are in the heart of the muddle. However much people talk about parenting being about nurture not nature, if a woman talks about having a baby, they assume she gave birth to it. If she didn't give birth to it, she's not really the mother, is she?

The further complication is that in order to make any kind of sense of what has been said so far, I have to come out as a lesbian. I suddenly realise that the person I'm talking to doesn't *know*. That it has never come up before. And that of course if they've not actively been told I'm a lesbian, they will assume I'm heterosexual. The middle of a casual conversation with a work colleague about the universally understood topic of babies is certainly not a place any sensible person would choose to embark on the thorny topic of lesbian identity. So the conversation founders, and I am left feeling exposed, vulnerable, and like a fraud in my claim to be Sam's mum.

The thing is, the easiest way for people to understand my relationship to Sam is for them to know that Ann and I are lovers. For us to break out of invisibility. Simple but scary, involving double doses of vulnerability. Lesbians get beaten up, get thrown out of their jobs, have their windows smashed. I didn't want that to happen to us. It was safer to hide behind people's assumption that my lover is my saintly sister giving up her chance of LIFE to dedicate herself to charity-case me, than to risk their response to the truth.

When Sam was a few weeks old, our cleaner of a year's standing left us. Desperation. There we were, wandering through life in that strange state of fuzzy shock and delight peculiar to first-time parents, when suddenly one of the mainstays of our support system was gone. We had to find someone else, quick. We discussed it. Wanted ads were put up in the local newsagents and supermarket, a date set for interviews and a list of topics to cover agreed. Yes, this was the perfect time to broach the subject, to set the arrangement off on the right foot. Our new cleaner would know from the start that Ann and I were lovers and that Sam was *our* son. Everything would be out in the open and if they didn't like it they wouldn't take the job. Fine words uttered whilst sitting together in the security of our living room and each other's understanding.

Our good intentions melted amidst the nervousness of sitting face to face with the actual person who might soon be poking into the intimacies of our bathroom and the bits that collect under our beds. We had to go through all the instructions that relate to me as a disabled person: 'This is how you operate the lift, don't be scared; put things back where you find them, they're probably there for a reason.' That was enough for all of us to handle. Ann and I tacitly agreed to avoid the other issue. Our need was too great, the risk too big.

So we carried on as before, allowing the question of our relationship to be passed over in the miasmic cloud which English people allow to obscure things they don't want to face. But having Sam had etched its significance more deeply and painfully in my life, and the price of this silence is now much higher.

This week Sam has invented a new game. A big cushion and a medium-sized cushion are arranged in the middle of the floor, then he dives into them and starts swimming. After a bit he turns to me, stretching out his arms and calling 'Help me, help me!' I get my helping hand and reach out to him with it. He grabs it and I haul him ashore. He gets up, gives me a look, and dives in again.

He's started to tuck Teddy into 'bed' on the settee for a midday nap. He does it with great care.

After a trip to the park and the duck pond, Sam lines his toy children up on the edge of my bath saying 'Dudu watch wadah'. I create some waves to make it more interesting for the children to watch.

In the first year of Sam's life, when he was just a few months old, I got so desperate in my isolation and confusion about what was happening to me, that I put an ad in the personal columns of *Spare Rib*. It cost me about ten quid, which at the time seemed like a lot of money, with only my half-time wages and Ann's dwindling maternity pay coming in. However, I thought it was a risk worth taking. The ad went something like 'Non-biological disabled mother seeks similar for experience-sharing and support'. Well, however much I might *feel* like I was the only one in the world, my reason told me there must be at least one other somewhere in Britain, and who knows, maybe more. On the one hand it seemed like a completely absurd ad to place, an absurd person to be even. Or perhaps it was just this pushing myself into the light of public day that seemed ridiculous. Perhaps it was okay to be this strange person as long as I stayed under that rock with the woodlice and other pale creepy crawlies. On the other hand the ad was like a brave little flag of hope, waving in the winds of the world, and saying 'I'm here, I'm here, wave your flag if you're there.'

The only reply I received arrived on a lovely summer's day. I was a bit on edge that day as my lift had broken down and I was stuck upstairs. I was sitting in Sam's sunny room, playing with him, when the letter and a friend arrived simultaneously: the friend for lunch, the letter as the potential fulfilment of all the hopes that no one in my immediate circle could answer. There was something about the letter that made it instantly recognisable – I can't remember what the signs were, but I *knew*. My heart leapt and fluttered. I would have liked to have gone off to a private place to open my letter, but here was my friend, come to be sociable and eat with us in her squeezed one-hour lunchbreak. I couldn't just leave her sitting there with her tuna barm and fizzy orange. On the other hand I couldn't ignore the letter either. It pulsated with possibilities. It held my fate in its folds. Was I about to be introduced to the woman who would shed the light of clarity on my experience? Become a bosom friend for the rest of my life? Would it be me and her against the world?

So I opened the letter. There and then. Wouldn't you have done the same?

'... athletic outdoor woman who enjoys hill-walking, climbing and water-sports. Available for camping holiday in France any week in August.' Was this some kind of hideous joke? Had I revealed my need, made myself vulnerable, only to receive this punch in the guts? This woman and myself were probably the two most mismatched of *Spare Rib*'s entire readership. Should I reply to her – 'Would love to come camping but at present I'm stuck upstairs in my three bedroomed semi in suburban Chorlton. Perhaps when the lift is mended . . .'?

I was stunned, but it wouldn't have been polite to burst into tears, or rage round the room, or tear the letter to shreds. It would have upset Sam and anyway I was supposed to be entertaining a friend. I registered my shock and disappointment then carried on munching my ham roll and crisps. Meanwhile the awful letter burned a hole in my pocket.

Closer examination of the letter and the latest issue of *Spare Rib* revealed what had happened. My correspondent had been replying not to me but to the athletic outdoor type whose ad had appeared above mine and who wanted a female companion for a French camping holiday. She'd just put the wrong reference number on the letter. It was a mistake. I was bereft. Perhaps she didn't exist then, this person who was going through the same things as me. Or perhaps she was so sussed out she felt no need to reach out. Or perhaps she just didn't read *Spare Rib* that week. Who knows? In any event, I never heard from her. I had to do without. And I did.

Sam, sitting on my bed, picks up my novel, opens it, and starts to read, 'Big baaad wolf; biiiig, baaaad wolf; big bad wolf.'

It is May and we are picnicking on a grassy slope. Sam is at the bottom. He fixes me with his eyes and runs remorselessly towards me, launching himself at me at the last moment. We tumble backwards, laughing, him on top, me underneath. Looking up I see his face an inch from mine, framed by blue sky. It is bursting with delight and triumph.

We have a bucketful of 'paper rain'; torn-up newspaper that everyone threw over each other at Sam's second birthday party. Two months later he finds it, three minutes before teatime, and empties it on the living room floor. He shuffles through it, jumps into it, kicks it into the air.

Sam is my son.

Jeni Fulton

Journey

At first glance it must seem so ordinary. The two of us sitting here in the car, speeding along the motorway. The man driving. The woman in the passenger seat. Him giving me a lift home after a weekend with friends.

The windscreen wipers scrape slices off the damp drizzliness outside. The world looks blurred at the edges. The fog hangs, heavy, chill, clinging.

But no matter. It suits me very well, in fact – perhaps the smothering mist will slow this journey down, and give me longer with him.

As the car slides on through the wetness there is an insistent hissing of tyres on tarmac, wheels in water. Other vehicles pass in the middle lane, with an irregular whoosh, spattering our view with their greasy spray. I'm conscious of the rhythmic clack and squeak of the hard-worked wipers.

We laugh, share a joke. Exchange smiles and chat. I lean forward and, after brief negotiation, change the cassette. There's something warm and full about the music as it swirls around inside the car. He suddenly sings two lines out loud with the band, at the top of his voice: a discordant parody. We laugh again.

'Do you remember when we played this at . . .?' Two people with a long joint history, apparently entirely comfortable in each other's company.

But it's not quite like that. Nor is this the stuff of wild, unbridled love. No, this is something altogether more familiar, placid, homely perhaps. Something with an easy and even solidity, without the intensity and excesses associated with passionate relationships. This is surely the contented companionship of friends? The problem is, that's not all I want.

Out of the corner of my eye, I watch him straightening out his arms, as if to push away the steering wheel. Arching his back, catlike stretching, into the enclosed seat. Shoving the sleeves of his sweatshirt up his arms, slowly, one after the other. Forearms fanning the flames of lust? Quite absurd.

He is very comfortable with his body. He is able to bare it to the world, apparently without a second thought. He loves the sun, so he's down to his shorts and basking happily in the warmth at the earliest summer opportunity. I've seen that often enough. Lucky old me – discerning and appreciative spectator. We sat on the beach together last year enjoying the sunshine. Only I was fully clothed, of course; I couldn't strip off in front of him and all those people and go in for a swim, though I'd have loved to. I wonder what it would be like to be comfortable with my body.

We're still laughing. That's something we do a lot together. (There are other things I'd like to do a lot together, but I can't tell him about them.)

'Honestly, I just wish you'd been there – it was exactly your sort of occasion . . .' His hand squeezes my shoulder briefly. Just long enough to send that familiar electricity through me. It was so unexpected. Not unwelcome, of course, just unexpected. And minor, very minor – but I've learned to be grateful for even the smallest encounters. It's not that we don't touch each other: we hug in greeting and exchange pecks. At least – we did.

I can remember each occasion from the last ten years quite clearly. But somehow it seems there hasn't been anything for a long time. I think I must be in an advanced state of touch deprivation. Have I really withdrawn so far from situations of intimate contact? I've become afraid of people backing away – sensing, perhaps, the extreme discomfort I now feel about my own deteriorating body. I can only associate touch now with impersonal medical matters.

'Such an interesting case! Can I just feel . . .?'

I'm quite a tactile person. I am, aren't I? Well, I *was*. It hasn't always been like this. Suddenly, without warning, a clear picture flashes into my mind of the risk-taking young woman I once was. I remember that time – at seventeen – when I disposed of the encumbrance of virginity, with a sullen young man of sought-after good looks whose attentions flattered and excited me. At first, the innuendoes over the snooker table in the club room, long since deserted by friends who had gone off in search of the frisson of an under-age drink, leaving us to frissons of another kind. That was where it started: the peculiarly distasteful, unsatisfactory screws. A series of unpleasant yet compelling encounters, all in sordid places and in seamy situations. We never had to take all our clothes off. Just as well. He probably never fully realised . . . Though my body wasn't quite so bad then – and I certainly didn't hate it so much.

But I can't blame it all on unreconstructed or immature men. There are other memories which prove that I never really got to emotional grips with my situation. What about the unemployed social worker twelve years my senior? A wise old man of thirty-two. He was prepared to try to understand it, wanted to confront it, talk about it. Caressing hands? Or hands curiously feeling for scars? At least he thought about what I might want; it was I who didn't know how to talk about it, I who couldn't handle the openness and honesty. It was I who said 'Turn out the light'. Quite soon I ran away. I often wish all that could have happened ten years later.

But would I really have handled it any better later on? Then, I used to pretend that my body wasn't really the way it is. I took the risks and – mostly – got away with it. It was almost as if I'd disbelieved my deformities away. (Although with hindsight I wonder if I got what I really needed from those situations.) But now, I seem to have convinced myself that physical intimacy would be much more difficult, either because I know more about what I want and am less prepared to make risky compromises, or just because I'm more conscious of my body. As if the structural problems of that body were not sufficient impediment to romance, spontaneous lust, or even just close physical affection, more and more artificial appliances now hold me together. By the time all those had been cast aside, the flames of passion would be well and truly doused.

Disconcertingly, my unhappiness about my body has grown as I have become increasingly political about being a disabled person. In other areas of my life I have become more assertive and confident about who I am, an important part of which is me as a disabled woman. I am, after all, a woman with a happily independent life, a beautiful home, a ridiculously senior job. Yes, I can say proudly, that is me, despite the ways society tries to deny me the competence I have, tries to make me invisible, put me down, patronise me, exclude me, deny me my civil rights. Mostly I am strong enough to get politically angry, to challenge and continue to grow. Hard as it sometimes is, I really enjoy that part of the journey.

Then I see myself naked in the bathroom mirror, and suddenly that sight redefines me. I wonder if the politics help me avoid what I have to do in challenging my relationship with my emotional and physical self. I want to make progress in that relationship as I have done with my political self, but if I can't like my body, love it, be kind to it, how can I expect anyone else to feel differently about it? I'm so out of practice that I can't imagine what I would do now if I wanted to seduce someone. Others see, fancy and proposition – a usual course of events. I couldn't even approach that. I would have to embark on a full discussion – what my body is like, how I'm restricted, and so on . . . and so on . . . and so on. Some seduction! Or I could just grab the condoms from the bathroom cupboard (hoping they're not past their sell-by date – very likely by now, I'm afraid), and risk him recoiling in horror. Perhaps it would be easier with a relative stranger, rather than with a tried and trusted friend where there would be so much more to lose . . .

'Hello? Hello? . . . Are you still there?' I jerk back to the here and now, worried that my vivid thoughts have been written across my face. But no, he's acting quite normally and is simply repeating what he was saying while I was so far away.

Focusing on the grey-green sodden landscape slipping past the car helps bring me back to the present. To the me that I offer in this situation, with this person; to the part-me I have chosen to reveal. I am distanced now from the risks the younger me was once prepared to take, and somewhat awed by them. And I am frustrated at my inability to act and take the emotional initiative which I feel might break the deadlock I'm in. It feels like I've retreated under a shell – perhaps one day I'll wake up as a tortoise.

More mist. More miles. The road ahead divides. Choices, I think, choices. Which route to take. I have lapsed into silence again.

He half-turns his head momentarily, one eyebrow quizzically raised.

'You okay?'

Golden Opportunity swoops into the car and lands on the dashboard, staring me mercilessly in the face. 'Go on then,' it taunts, 'tell him that you're not okay, tell him how you really feel about him.' I hesitate – then smile and nod. Golden Opportunity melts out of the windscreen and is washed away by the rain.

Going in one direction means maintaining the status quo: saying nothing, and allowing this friendship to carry on, undeveloped, unchallenged – increasingly unsatisfactory? What would be the cost? Minimal, the martyr in my psyche tells me. Merely continued torment and turmoil, from top to toe, from inside out. No different from how it has been these past ten years. But emotional pain is so invisible. It is known only to me, and it has become so familiar after all this time. Like the physical pain, it is part of me. And, like the physical pain, it has to be bravely borne and certainly not mentioned. After all, I've worked so hard to be the strong, independent, coping woman. I can't show my weaknesses now.

What would happen if I took the other route? The path of honesty and of telling him the truth? What would be the consequences of that? It's terrifyingly unpredictable. I assume the worst, of course – rejection. He just doesn't see me as a sexual being. It would probably be the end of even what there is now. The quiet, relaxed comfortableness of being close. (Well, as close as friends can be when there's something so important that remains unsaid.) It isn't that I'm looking for wedding bells and happily-ever-afters. I'm too much of a cynic for that and, much more important, I revel in my domestic space and independence, my status as a singular woman. I'd never voluntarily give that up. I just want a physical and sexual dimension to this valuable friendship.

The car has stopped now. The rain has stopped too, but everything is sodden and heavy. The fog still clings everywhere. Time has stopped because I can't get past the point at which the motorway divides for me. I'm frustrated by the whole situation. I don't want things to go on as they are. I'm weary of emotional dishonesty, of being on my guard, of not being completely me, of suppressing such an important part of myself, of behaving so inconsistently, at odds with the strong political woman I am. But is it possible any more to be honest in talking affairs of the heart – or body, more's the point – when there's a fundamental, insuperable barrier between us? The twisted, scarred and sagging deformity that I perceive to be me.

There's so much further still to go.

Aspen

Bitter and Twisted

bitter?
yes, i am bitter
like acid, and
like poison fruit.
twisted?
yes, i am twisted,
like an old tree trunk
racked and gnarled
like old roots
twisting deep in the soil
i am here and i
will not be moved:
i am far too strong
and deadly.

Michele Wates

Self-Respect

Sensing the averted gaze of pity, she found herself preparing for the moment when they would pass one another on the narrow path. She could not help herself from wanting people, even complete strangers like this man, to notice that although she might be dragging herself along like a wounded animal her eyes were bright, she had a ready smile and her voice, if he should have reason to hear it, was up and out; confident.

Increasingly she asked herself why it should be necessary to put so much effort into convincing people that she was in good shape, psychically, if not physically. She heard herself telling her husband's aunt that 'the walking gets worse and worse and everything else gets better and better'. It wasn't that it was an untrue statement at that time, but why did she feel this compulsion to reassure?

Once, whilst carefully lowering herself down the perilous steps outside a friend's house, she saw that an elderly woman had stopped on the pavement and was making no secret of the fact that she was watching her. 'You've got gammy legs,' she stated matter of factly.

'Yes.'

'Poor you.'

'Yes.'

It was wonderfully refreshing for once to have the direct gaze and the open expression of sympathy. Even so it was completely automatic to make sure that an inflection of inner health was projected into her smiling replies.

Another time she fell and hurt herself just outside her own

front door. There was the shock and the blood and the pain of a dislocated finger. Above all there was the distress of having her own children standing at the door staring down at her in horror. 'I thought someone had tried to murder you,' said one. 'I wish you weren't disabled,' sobbed the other. She badly needed to cry and howl and shake, but instead she cast about for something ordinary to say in something that she hoped was close to her usual tone of voice. Needing to reassure, needing not to be rejected.

Maybe you had to risk being rejected in order to accept yourself finally. But where to start? The unknown man on the path between the car park and the school entrance seemed as good a place as any. Though his gaze was fastened on the door he was heading towards, she knew that he didn't miss a single detail of her precarious, slow progress. As they drew close to each other on the path she noticed herself making the habitual effort to relax her face muscles so that the strain of walking was less obvious. She deliberately let go of the compulsion to try and establish eye contact. She allowed herself to notice how she was feeling. She was feeling bad.

Anna Sullivan

Part of a Life

July 26th 1987, a warm, balmy night. I wake suddenly and hear footsteps, people running, shouting, 'Get out, get out, the house is on fire!' I throw on my dressing gown, for there's no time for anything else. We cannot use the phone – it's in the middle of the fire which is raging through the centre of the house. The dog is howling, the fur burnt off her back. My son is in the passage with his girlfriend, both wearing coats over their bare bodies, and we fall out into the street, now full of people. My neighbours opposite have called the fire brigade but before they arrive the front windows explode. The sound is terrible. It is three o'clock in the morning, and as bright as day. My son tells the fire chief that the fire was started with petrol bombs, he heard the smashing glass, and the explosion of the ignited petrol. I stand watching my house burn and feel completely frozen. I am not crying, just shaking so much that I have to sit down and hold my body together with my arms. My neighbours offer me whisky. The smell is repellent to me, but I drink three glasses and am sick all next day. The middle section of my house is a charred shell, all my books, my paintings, the fragments of my life, have perished in the flames.

The next day the police are all over the place, foraging around asking questions. They have found the remains of four petrol bombs amongst the wrecked furniture and burnt carpets. 'Who hates you this much?' they ask me. I tell them what I think, that it is the work of fascists. They feign disbelief and say aggressively, 'Well, if you're mixed up in that kind of thing you probably brought it on yourself.' Because of my anti-racist activity the fascists have threatened to kill me many times, now they have destroyed a part of me.

Eight months later I get up to go to work. I am on a year's secondment to train as an Art Therapist. For years I have been a classroom teacher, and I have waited a long time for this opportunity. The journey to Goldsmiths' College is long and exhausting. My legs feel like lead weights and the pain is terrible. I am so tired. I haven't slept one night since the fire without waking at three in the morning in terror. When I arrive at the Art Therapy Unit I try to walk up the stairs but my legs won't work. I sit on the stairs and give up. Someone takes me home in a car. I never go back. A few months later I am diagnosed with ME.

December 1984. My father is dying. The man I have adored all my life lies fragile and shrunken, propped up on pillows. He looks so small. My body feels like it has no insides, my face muscles are rigid, my back ramrod straight in the hospital chair. He lies in a coma, his breathing laboured and rasping. I sit on one side of his bed, my sister on the other. We each hold one of his hands and we are linked together like this for the next ten hours until he leaves us. Earlier in the day my children had been with me and had said goodbye to their grandfather. My daughter Miriam, who is a nurse, had cared for him the previous day and night. But now there are just the three of us. For a time there is also my ex-husband who, although he didn't love me for long, never stopped loving my father. He cannot arrange his face properly and sits large and uncomfortable or paces the small room clasping and unclasping his hands. All through the night my sister and I talk to each other, recalling our childhood and my father's life, how much he gave to us and everyone who knew him. We talk about our mother who had died two years before. He had never got over it. He loved her intensely right to the end. I still believe that his grief killed him.

I was brought up by parents who believed in fighting for a better life. They taught me that being working class meant being proud and standing up for what you believed in. My father used to tell me wonderful stories about growing up in the East End of London; about everything he had been involved in in the twenties and thirties. He told me about the battle against Mosley and his blackshirts at Cable Street and Ridley Road, and how my mother used to bail him out with her rent book every time he was arrested. He was involved in the International Brigade during the Spanish civil war, and was part of the unemployed workers' movement in Hackney. I listened to these stories and I wanted to be like him. But above all, my parents gave me love, and showed me that without it nothing works. All night my sister and I sat talking, while his breathing became more ragged. We talked and we couldn't stop, but we never let go of his hands.

He died just before dawn. My sister threw herself over his body, sobbing and calling his name. I stayed still, my body like a board, a terrible pain in my throat. I kissed him for the last time and my inner voice said, 'Don't cry or you'll never stop, don't lose control.'

I didn't begin to let go and grieve for him until four years later when I was in hospital in a special unit for ME patients.

October 1988. The ward has eight beds in it and I am given one in the corner. I feel detached and empty, my legs hurt and I can hardly walk. There are other women in the room. Some have curtains drawn around them and are sleeping. The doctors here believe that people with ME are so exhausted that their bodies can't heal. (I know that this place offers me the only hope so far.) My life is wrecked, in ruins, I can't see who I am any more. My body is a conductor of pain. I have been fainting and falling down in the street for months now and the pains in my limbs never let up. Violent headaches wake me in the middle of the night and vertigo makes my world terrifying. My life is a nightmare of pain and fear. I am drowning. But none of this shows on the outside. I pride myself on my stoicism.

A nurse takes me to undress and get into bed, the doctor is coming. The first sight of him startles me. He is wearing a black kippah on his head and has a full beard, but behind the beard a young face. He's Jewish and very religious. I like the doctor's voice. He introduces himself, asks a few questions. Suddenly he says, 'Do you always wear makeup?' I feel exposed, vulnerable, and rage boils up inside me. I shout at him, 'How dare you ask such a question? Are you judging me by the way I look? What do you know of my life?' He stares at me in horror and walks out of the ward. Well, I might as well go home. I feel stricken, incredibly upset. Suddenly he is there in front of me again. 'Forgive me,' he says, 'I didn't mean to hurt you.' So I stay. He sits next to me and we talk. I am amazed at how he listens. Doctors don't usually listen, not for long anyway. He tells me what he thinks. That my body is worn out, has given up. That a lot of my physical illnesses have been caused by stress and emotional trauma. That I have pushed myself to the extremes of exhaustion. He doesn't tell me that I am foolish, that I have been wrong. He seems to understand why I have been committed to a political life. Why I have done things that are dangerous. I tell him about my three children and that they are my great love. He doesn't make me feel that I am to blame for what has happened to me. He tells me that I am very ill but that in order to even begin to heal my body I must rest and sleep. I must forget all the things that I think I ought to be doing. I think I can trust this man. He seems to be trying to understand my life.

For the next three weeks I drift in and out of deep sleep. A young girl in the next bed lies behind her blue curtains and weeps. Her life has hardly begun. My eldest daughter, Sharon, comes to see my every day. Twelve miles on public transport in cold grey weather. Sometimes I'm so tired I can hardly talk to her so she sits up on my bed and holds me. I see my doctor every day and when I have enough energy we talk about music and politics and art, all the things that have been important in my life. He thinks I should have my art materials brought in so that I can paint. My body doesn't hurt so much but my legs are getting worse.

I have been here a month. My doctor asks me if I would like to go to dance therapy. Yes, I'll go. I'll put on proper clothes and feel better. But how can I dance when I can't walk? You'll see, he says.

I am in a room full of strangers. We borrow some of my tapes because the music therapist has not turned up. The occupational therapist who has been to the session many times says she'll take it over, so we begin. Because many of us have been immobile for so long the session is meant to loosen up our bodies, using music as an emotional trigger as well as a relaxation technique. We put on a tape which says Mozart on the sleeve, but it isn't. It's a Beethoven string quartet, the slow movement. I haven't heard this music for twenty years and I am transfixed, frozen, but nobody realises. My heart is racing, out of control. I want to shout 'Turn it off, I can't bear it', but I don't. I am silent, lost, somewhere else.

It is night time. The ward is silent, except for the usual noises of sleep. The blue curtains enclose me like a tomb. I pull the table over my bed and get out my paints. I stare at the blank page. The music is still in my head and I have a terrible compulsion to hear the Beethoven quartet again. I put on the headphones and listen. The music unlocks the door to a memory I thought I had buried long ago. I cry and I cannot stop. I cry for the young woman I was then, for grief at the loss of the man I had loved. I weep so much my body aches with it. I am terrified. How can I stop? I try to paint it out of me, but the paint on the page is transparent. The face I have painted is emptied by grief, like me.

I don't see my doctor for two days. He never works on Shabbat but comes in on Sundays. I am still crying when he comes to see me and because I can't speak to him I have written down what has happened. He sits on my bed and holds my hand while I cry and says he will get me a room on my own so that I can grieve in peace; that my body is finally freeing itself of the steel girders that I've wrapped around it to hold in my pain. He says that this is a beginning.

I stayed in my room for three months, in a part of the cardiology unit. This was a difficult time for my children. I had always been strong because I had had to be. I wanted them still to see me as that strong mother even now when I was weak and sad. I was afraid of their fear.

I painted forty pictures and wrote every day. It was like lifting the lid off a boiling pot. I grieved for my father at last.

It is nearly three years since I left hospital. At first, although much better, I couldn't walk more than a few steps, and for six months I suffered extreme pain all over my body. My children were always there and sometimes when I really felt that I couldn't face another day feeling the way I did, my women friends would sit with me all through the night until the bad time passed.

Until a year ago I still saw my doctor, then the unit was closed down. I had been so lucky to be treated there. So many ME sufferers are treated as neurotic hypochondriacs, because the condition is still not diagnosible by standard medical practices. Myalgic Encephalomyelitis has been derided as 'yuppie flu' in the press, so people are afraid to talk about the emotional and psychological factors that have led to their conditions. The fact is that ME is a very painful physical condition – a result of our immune system's failure to work fully. Viruses invade our bodies, and the muscle pain and exhaustion are never-ending. We must all find our own way to deal with ME – many change their diet or use homeopathic methods.

I faced the traumas in my life which had left my body so vulnerable. My doctor had shown me that I could change my life and not feel guilty about all the things I could no longer do. That I should care about myself and listen to what my body tells me. Sometimes I feel full of energy and think that I can do anything, but it doesn't last long. I accept that I am disabled and have to live my life at a different speed. Some of the rewards are that I have time to paint and write, time to enjoy my grandchildren. The rise of fascism again, and the many terrible things that are happening in the world, make me feel that I should be out and about organising, but I know that I can't do it any more. Then I feel depressed and angry. When this happens I think back to my time in hospital. I used to see a hypnotherapist who taught me how to relax completely and how to breathe properly again. He would ask me to think of the most beautiful place or situation that I would like to be in at that moment.

This is what I saw. A week after the fire I went to Israel to see my daughter who was living on a kibbutz. It was a foolish thing for me to have done because I was so ill, but I travelled with a woman friend and we arrived in the early hours of the morning. Tel Aviv in summer is suffocatingly hot and humid but I hadn't realised how near to the sea the city is. At five in the morning, as soon as it was light, we left our hotel, and when we turned the corner of the street there it was, the sea. Bluer than I have ever seen it, rolling into miles of golden sand. The sun, blood red, glowed behind a heat haze that hung over the water. We found two deckchairs and we sat by the edge of the sea and while it lapped around our feet, we watched the sun rise.

Ann Macfarlane

Loss

I feel teardrops trickle through
   nearly half a century
For the loss of touch.
Is it something gentle,
   warm, intimate, exciting,
Being touched?
Does it contribute towards
   that feeling of
Being loved?
I taste the saltiness of tears
   engulfing the years
For the loss of sexuality.
Is it something sensual,
   self-defined, empowering?
Does it allow the sensitivity
   of being a woman
To be acknowledged?
I expose a stormy outburst of emotion
   marking almost half a century
   of anger
For the loss of relationships.
Are they something experienced only
   by non-disabled people?
Belonging, being welcomed as
   part of family, community, society?

Let me give expression to
Almost a lifespan
of isolation, of painful separations.
Let me not be ashamed in grieving
for the loss of touch,
love, sexuality, personal growth
As I search and reach out
for inclusion.

PART THREE

Jenni Meredith

Are you **D**eaf?

Are you bl**I**nd?

Can't you **S**ee me?

Can't you he**A**r me?

And do you **B**lame

my disab**I**lity

for your **L**ack

of ins**I**ght,

for your shor**T**comings?

Do **Y**ou?

Pam Mason

Agoraphobia: Letting Go

When I was five years old, I thought I was possessed by the Devil.

The Devil wasn't there all the time. He usually arrived in the school holidays, the only guest we ever had in our house, turning up when I was bored, when the family relationships had begun to crack under the strain of us all being shut up together, day after day. There were no trips to the cinema or walks to the park. We just all sat there separately, in front of the TV.

He usually came at night when I was in bed. My mind would wander, my self-control would slip, and He would slide into my head, splitting me in two, turning the world wildly surreal, as if it was another planet, a place bizarre beyond the scope of science fiction. When the Devil had me, I did not even recognise my own body: what were these white tubes of flesh that imprisoned me? When the Devil came, I wanted to shrug off body, self, experience, everything, and evaporate into space.

But the other part of me wanted to kill the Devil and be an ordinary little girl again, and that part always won, though each victory seemed like a miracle. I would scream for my mother. Even though there was normally some hostility between us, my mother was the only one who could make it better. 'You shouldn't think so much,' she'd say to me, and I agreed. But how could I stop?

I knew I was the only person in the world who had this. I called it That Feeling, but I collected other (inaccurate) scare-words over the years: mad, schizophrenic; 'in the head', 'neurotic', 'head the ball' if you want to be Scouse about it. I never ruled out demonic possession. I hadn't been in a Catholic church since I was christened, but perhaps I got Catholicism by osmosis. I remember being about ten or eleven, sitting with my friend, playing with dolls on the kitchen floor in her house, thinking how outraged her mother would be if she knew that a consort of Satan was in the house. And I feared dying because I knew what Hell was: That Feeling, for all eternity.

I couldn't tell anyone about it, not properly. I knew that if I ever did describe it accurately to anyone, they would get it too, and their lives would be ruined.

No one outside the house noticed anything much, except that I had what is now called school phobia, and that I was a very quiet child. But I did well academically, and at sixteen I was preparing to sit ten O levels.

And then That Feeling started happening in the classroom. Reality would swim horribly around me, and I longed to get up and run away home.

My mother called the doctor. He came to the house. 'What's the matter?' he said, tired, irritable. 'I don't know,' I said, smiling, with all the embarrassed incoherence of sixteen.

He wrote a prescription for Ativan. He carried on writing prescriptions for Ativan for the next eight years. Little blue tablets, crumbly on the tongue, instant salvation, the hammer to the Devil. Immense relief, and then, all too soon, the agony of waiting for it to be time to take the next one. They worked wonderfully at first, but after a while taking them had no effect on me, except to add addiction to my other worries.

I was preparing for my A levels, dreaming of studying English at Liverpool University. None of our family had ever been to university before. I was to be the first. If all went well.

But terrible things were happening at home, inexplicable, frightening things. People very close to me, driven by their own sadnesses, were trying to harm themselves. Although I thought I was coping perfectly, That Feeling was swooping down on me with increasing regularity. I had no one to tell it all to – my best friend had just discovered boys and I no longer felt close enough to her. So, I threw myself into my schoolwork, convincing myself that I was fine, in spite of everything. I did my homework, wrote my essays, asked questions in class. And when That Feeling swooped down during lessons as if I was Tippi Hedren in *The Birds*, I would scribble notes frantically to keep it from completely engulfing me. That helped with my work anyway, so what was there to worry about?

But I began to feel frightened of being away from familiar people, familiar places. When I was seventeen, I had gone to London with the school. At eighteen I was afraid to go, afraid of That Feeling possessing me when I was hundreds of miles from home and help. I missed open days at Sheffield and Hull Universities because I was frightened of the journeys.

Then, one Saturday night, I was sitting in front of the fire reading *The Grapes of Wrath* when it happened to me. The Devil, or whatever it was, took full possession of me. I began to scream and I couldn't stop, the Feeling was so terrible. They called a doctor, a man I'd never seen before. He looked at me with terrible pity, insisted that I go and see a psychiatrist and gave me some sleeping pills.

I didn't see the psychiatrist because she was in Whiston and I was too scared to go so far from home and she wouldn't make house calls. But I did get repeat prescriptions for the sleeping tablets.

Before long I found the thought of going to Liverpool city centre, only seven miles away, a place I loved more than anywhere else in the world, too hard to imagine. And then Huyton Village, a quarter of a mile away, became too far. School was about three hundred yards down the road – somehow I got there during the last few weeks. I got through all my exams, breaking down on the last day, but battling on, doing the papers, getting some good marks, incredibly.

And then I just collapsed. It was a struggle to get as far as the garden gate.

By now I realised I had a form of agoraphobia. I fought. I made myself go out of the house, brief and terrifying as such trips were. Although Mum was fighting her own problems at the time, she offered to go out with me. This meant I could get further from the house and the freedom was as precious to me as it would be to any prisoner travelling under escort. But instead of curing our problems, we had pooled them. I became acutely dependent on her. We acted out the roles of extremely protective mother and sick, frightened toddler. She had to be there all the time now, to hold me and save me when That Feeling came, as it often did, blasting away at my self and all my hope. How could I ever live a normal life when I had this in my head? I read Claire Weekes' books and Open Door newsletters, desperate for a solution, but only terrified myself with other people's symptoms.

But agoraphobics sometimes take chances, shock themselves with their own achievements. I did this in 1982, when I tried to take up a place at Bangor University.

My mother and I stayed there for three days, three days when I couldn't eat and certainly couldn't go out alone, before we conceded defeat.

At home, I saw another doctor and insisted on being given better help.

And he referred me to a trainee psychologist who was prepared to do home visits.

Jacqui, her name was, a pretty young woman with a mass of hair and a slight Birmingham accent. She came to the house and together we teased out some strands of my life. I began to see that this agoraphobia hadn't just come down on me like a thunderbolt, but was the result of years of pressure, twisting my mind out of shape so that nothing was where it should be any more. Together, we began to name the Devil.

Jacqui took up a post with the Liverpool Health Authorities and, after a lot of agony and fear, I got into a taxi (with my mother) and we went to Fazakerley Hospital to see her.

I saw her twice a week, for several years, at Fazakerley and

Walton Hospitals. And afterwards, Mum and I would get a taxi into Town, into Liverpool, and just being there was heaven. The long wide streets, the old buildings, the Mersey, all the sites of the struggles of my ancestors, Catholic and Protestant, of the workers, of those fierce, fighting women, the ghosts blowing round the corners of St George's Hall and London Road, whom I could sense, but whose names I would not learn for many years yet.

Jacqui and I were uncovering everything, every patch of misery and fear, every manifestation of the Devil in my life.

The years passed like this, and it could have gone on forever probably: I'd heard all those horror stories about agoraphobics who stay indoors for decades. People think it isn't curable. Would I ever leave home, I used to wonder, would I ever be able to go out without my mother? Jacqui was sure I could, anyway.

I had made up my mind that I had to go to university, to get so far away that there would be no going back, no chance of getting a lift home in the first week. I chose Exeter, Brighton, Norwich. Before that, I hadn't even known where those places were, except that they were vaguely 'down south'. I looked at the map in the front of my new 1985 diary and I could hardly believe that places so far away from home could exist.

I remember the interviews, the journeys, long tunnels of winter darkness, the long drab nightmare of late-night trains, changing platforms, pitch-dark stations floating in a nowhere dotted with stars and red-and-green lights.

I was terrified of the journey (three hundred miles, via London) to Norwich. So I didn't go. I phoned and made an excuse. And they offered me a place, unconditionally.

I couldn't believe it. I still can't. I used to sit and wait for them to write back and say, sorry, there's been a mistake, we meant to give it to someone else. But in October 1985 Jacqui met me on Lime Street Station and I boarded the London train alone. My mother was seven miles away, twenty miles, a hundred, two hundred.

Crossing London, I shared a taxi with a Russian woman, who

told me that her mother had been far too stern and restrictive with her. 'So I gave my daughter a lot of freedom,' she said wryly, 'and now she says I don't love her.'

From Liverpool Street, I took the train through East Anglia, through the wide, bright fields which stretched to the horizon. The light was hot, everything was strange after the north – no cities, no towns, no big rivers.

And I got there. And I stayed. And I got my degree.

I'd like to be able to say it was all gloriously easy, but it wasn't. I was anorexic, obsessive, I got into all sorts of difficulties. After all, I had spent all my time from eighteen to twenty-four locked in the house or beside my mother, and I knew very little of life. I'd like to be able to say I'm fine now, but I'm not. I still have eating disorders, still get agoraphobic at times of stress, and I suffer from depression badly. But I think that this is to be expected. You can't spend twenty-odd years of your life thinking you're possessed, fearing death and hell every second, without being scarred by it.

But physically, I am free. I get around town without thinking about it much, I look after myself, I no longer have that (mutually) awful dependence on my mother.

I fought for my freedom, but I had a lot of help. And a lot of luck. It takes my breath away now, thinking how lucky I was: lucky to be educated enough to get to university, lucky to be offered a place like that, lucky to find a psychologist who was so adaptable and so good at her job.

All this happened in the early 1980s. Can agoraphobics still get home visits and intense attention on the NHS? I had a full student grant, and in those days students could still claim dole and housing benefit in vacations. That was vital: it was essential, for my sanity and my survival, that I did not go home between university terms. Agoraphobia is a disease incubated, hatched and sustained in unhealthy families. What do agoraphobics do about leaving home nowadays, when student grants are inadequate and students can't claim any money during vacations? Where do agoraphobics go if they can't get to college, when there are no council flats and housing association lists are years long and few landlords will let rooms to the unwaged and suitable special homes can be counted on the fingers of one hand?

It makes me furious that the escape routes I took have been closed off by government cuts.

Becoming free was all about learning about myself. What I once thought was the Devil was, mainly, anger: absolute burning fury about the way my life was, about the things that were happening to me. Like most women, I had learned to eat my own anger, not let it show. Suppressed and feared, it became concentrated, and sought expression in ways that terrified me. That Feeling was a bundle of 'wrong' emotions: anger, fear, need, love. I still get That Feeling. When I am most brave, I do not fight That Feeling, and though the feeling of dissolving is frightening, at the heart of it I always find a vital message.

I feel now that this is part of my life's work: letting go when That Feeling comes, and learning from it. Not fighting feels dreadful, almost impossible, like staying in the saddle of a bolting horse or not yanking your hands away from flames. Agoraphobics are prisoners of fear. I want all agoraphobics and all women to know that fulfilment lies in passing bravely *through* fear. At times I can be cowardly. But I now know what I want, and need, my life to be.

Kate Bromfield

'My Brilliant Career!'

September 1972
Start first job as an English teacher in a large inner city comprehensive school. Within a few weeks begin to have dizzy spells, periods of complete exhaustion, migraine. Attribute physical state to the stresses of work. Carry on.

April 1973
Get married. Move to a new flat. Experience tingling sensations in arms and legs, numb face, exhaustion. Doctor writes on certificate 'Nervous debility'. Three weeks off work.

August 1974
Move to a new house which needs a lot of work. I am curtain-making, decorating, teaching full-time, going to evening classes, leading a busy social life.

October 1974
Am walking up the hill to work one morning facing directly into the sun. Suddenly lights flash in my left eye. Think it's a migraine, continue to work. Vision goes in my eye leaving a grey blur. I go home and see the doctor. After a week on medication, eyesight returns. Go back to work.

February 1975
A few hours before our housewarming party for a hundred people, the vision goes in my right eye. I am shaky and my head hurts. Cannot cancel at such short notice. The following

afternoon, hung over and wobbly, walk with my sister to the casualty department of the local hospital. See neurologist. Tests, tests, tests. Multiple sclerosis diagnosed. Condition deteriorates, am off work for three months. Eyesight does not improve, am left with a small amount of peripheral vision in my right eye. Left eye, thankfully, okay.

April 1975
Return to work. Incredibly. ACTH injections have resulted in my losing three stone in weight. Now eight and a half stone and five feet nine, I have an entirely new self-image to come to terms with! People at work seem happy to discuss my new figure. I don't know how to begin to discuss anything else. I am still very weak and shaky, have frequent attacks of vertigo. I change to part-time work.

1978
We have decided to have children. We have had conflicting advice, often unsolicited, as to whether or not this is wise, but my health has been reasonably stable. Thirteen weeks into the pregnancy I develop German measles. I have two weeks off work. After much agonised discussion and on my doctor's advice we decide to continue with the pregnancy. I develop very high blood pressure, begin maternity leave as soon as I can. I am taken into hospital at thirty-two weeks, on enforced bedrest.

October 23rd, 1978
Emily is born. She is beautiful.

April 1979
Return to work. Childcare arrangements are not ideal but there is no choice – we have to pay the mortgage. I am exhausted to the extent that I frequently forget arrangements, cannot follow discussions. My face and body are numb. I often have pins and needles in my tongue.

October 1979
Emily has her first febrile convulsion. We had gone to work,

knowing that she was slightly unwell, but thinking that she was teething. I stay with her in hospital for a week. She is treated with phenobarbitone which makes her hyperactive. She hardly sleeps, day or night. Neither do we! I start to get debilitating palpitation attacks, some of which last for more than three hours at a time without stopping. I am given tablets. They are usually effective.

December 1979
I decide to give up work. Mark has a new job. We will just about be able to manage without my income. I hate being dependent on him financially. So much for independent woman! I become pregnant again. Emily has another febrile convulsion. She is in hospital for ten days. This time Mark and I take turns to be with her.

December 9th, 1980
Joe is born. He is beautiful too.

1981–1984
I experience what I now think was postnatal depression. I am always exhausted, tearful, very self-critical. Once I hit Emily on the back and bruise her. I can't talk to anyone, don't want to see anyone. My palpitation attacks become worse and more frequent. I begin to pass out with them. My GP tells me that the cause is Wolff-Parkinson-White syndrome, a condition which can be exacerbated by stress. 'I didn't tell you before because I thought you had enough to cope with already,' he says. I start new medication. It seems to work. But I am very numb and shaky and I am very low, my self-esteem is nil. A locum GP suggests that I ask for help. I hadn't realised that help was available! The local day nursery, now closed because of cuts, agrees to look after Joe on days when I am too ill to cope. I arrange to help them whenever I feel able. Most valuable of all, I have counselling for eighteen months.

1984

I begin to learn to take control over my life, so far as I am able. I learn when to say no, to make demands sometimes, to make some time for me. I have developed a passionate interest in early childhood education and take a two-year postgraduate diploma course. Although I have not officially retrained as a nursery teacher, I manage to persuade the inspector for nursery education to appoint me part-time. It is my first proper job in several years (paid work, that is!) and it is a lovely school. I am sometimes unwell, and the children are too, but the staff are great and we support each other.

We have moved to a new house. I am elected as a parent governor at the children's school. I am on a high.

January 1988

I start a new job. It is in a nursery class much closer to home, working with a teacher who has an outstanding professional reputation. I have been chosen from five applicants and my previous head had refused to release me for a term. I feel very confident.

Two days into the term, my childminder says she can no longer look after the children before and after school. She has given me one day's notice. The following morning Mark crashes on black ice. He is fine, but the car is a write-off. This is not a good start! Although the school is nearer to home, the journey is, in fact, more complicated than my previous one. The traffic jams are appalling and it is too far for me to walk without needing a rest on arrival. I have to take the kids to school first. I am in a constant state of tension. My workdays are spread throughout the week, Monday, Wednesday and Friday afternoon, and I quickly become very tired. It is difficult for me to get to know the children and the classroom. I realise, too, that I am expected to work 'for' rather than 'with' the nursery teacher. Our views on nursery education are very different. I begin to lose confidence.

One morning the head calls me into her room. 'Kath (she has never called me this before!), I feel I must tell you, dear (she's never called me this before either!), I know all about you.' She is obviously uncomfortable and I don't know what to say. *All* about me, I hope not! She tells me that she thinks I'm wonderful, that she has a relative with MS who just sits around in a wheelchair all day watching television. I say a little about how MS affects different people in different ways but it's difficult. I have to try and make my own situation clear when I'm not that clear about it myself! She is very kind. She offers me a lift back from work every evening. But our relationship has changed subtly, has become less professional. She makes jokes about my size, about my hairiness. She comments when my hands shake. She also asks me constantly to do supply work when I had explained clearly, so I thought, that although we need the money I also need rest! I begin to look for another job.

April 1989
I have cysts on my ovaries. I have a D and C.

I am offered a new job, a job-share this time, starting in September 1989. I am both apprehensive and excited.

June 10th, 1989
I am forty!

The summer is exceptionally hot. Several times, walking from the bus to work, I have such severe vertigo attacks that I have to sit down. The vision in my good eye is blurred. I start calling the children by the wrong names. I can't find things in the classroom. I drop things. I have cramps, numbness, pins and needles. If I move suddenly I overbalance. The staff in the nursery are very supportive but after a couple of weeks I realise that I have to give in, go home, see the doctor. I go to see the head. I am distressed, apologetic, mumble something about 'hope you don't feel I'm a liability'.

'Well,' she says, 'certainly, when I employ another part-timer I will have it written into her contract that she does supply when necessary ... You're very shaky, go home.'

After I have seen the doctor, I phone to tell the head that I am likely to be off work for some time. 'I'm just going to a meeting,' she says, 'I can't talk now', and puts the phone down. We have not communicated since. I sent my certificates to her secretary.

September 1989
I begin the new job still not fully recovered. It's a nice school but a very challenging one. Some of the children are difficult, some of the staff are, well, difficult, too! I'm having incontinence problems, have to spend a lot of time in the loo.

April 1990
Slipped disc in lower back. The pain is excruciating, like child-birth but without the rewards. Mark has to lift me on to a bedpan. I *hate* this lack of privacy, *hate* this dependence. I'm desperate to wash my hair but we can't work out how to do it as I can't stand without passing out. Osteopathy is helping, but it costs a lot. I am aware that only a few people can afford it. My hip keeps locking so that I can hardly walk. My school is sending my class home. I have a recurring nightmare. I am the character in *O Lucky Man!* – human head, animal body under the sheet. I feel a 'non' person, worthless.

July 1990
I return to work, having asked for a transfer to another school, one day a week with supply when necessary.

November 1990
New school. Another slipped disc. Quicker recovery.

April 1991
Slipped disc again. Again I cannot walk. My left leg and foot have gone numb. Is this caused by the disc or MS? I have been paying superannuation. My GP is very supportive. 'Yours is a unique situation and you really mustn't try to push yourself if you don't feel you can,' she says. I apply for, and am granted, early retirement from teaching on health grounds. I am forty-two.

Entry from my journal July 1992

What a lot of things have changed and some of them for the better! My back has not totally recovered, is still painful at times, and my left leg is still weak and the foot numb. I am more mobile now. I am beginning to get out and go where I please, although I still move very slowly. But it is not just a question of mobility. I'm beginning to feel again that I can function as a responsible adult, in spite of illness, that my lifestyle can be as viable as anyone else's.

As I write this now I am angry, not for myself, but for others. For most of my adult life I have moved between being independent and dependent, between 'ability' and 'disability'. I have the support of family, some very special friends and a lovely GP. I have worked. I am entitled to a pension and invalidity benefit. I have the chance to take stock, to begin again. Other women, and men too, have none of these advantages and in the current political climate are being neglected and ignored. Those of us who can must fight for them, must write for them. They must not become invisible.

Eve Goss

All Lost?

She *was* my friend
Because she came to see me when few others did
And she brought me food and medicine I needed.
But when I asked her to write my poems down
She laughed a spiteful laugh
And did not write for me.

And the poems in my head
Are no longer in my head.
The vision that the streaming fire of agony
Searing along my spine gave to me,
That barbed wire packed inside my pelvis
Gave to me, is gone.
But I remember saying to this friend
(She *was* a friend)
That there was something I longed to tell others
And she laughed at me
And told me about writing she was doing for the church.

I was so full of poetry
While I was in that strange land of pain.
What discoveries had I made, What mysteries unveiled?
Are they all lost?
Now I have this memory that for years
While I was ill,
I had no friend who would write down what I could not.

Maybe, if I write this down, one day
Someone who lies weak and alone
With water of wisdom welling up
Will find a hand to cup it out for others
So all will not be lost.

Gohar Kordi

I Was Touched

I entered the writing class and sat next to the tutor. 'My name is Yvonne,' she said, shaking my hand warmly, and she asked everyone to introduce themselves and say why they were there. Later I learned that this introduction was just for me as I had been half an hour late. I was touched. When you cannot see, these things matter.

Each time Yvonne spoke to me she turned to me and touched me on the arm, as if because she could not have eye contact with me, she touched me instead. I felt special. Something in her touch and her voice made me feel comfortable, safe.

During the break I talked to the woman sitting next to me on the other side. We stayed in the classroom, chatting away, the two of us. We talked about being from a different country with a different culture – she from South Africa and me from Iran. Totally different societies from the one we are living in now. Troubled countries. Touchy subject. We identified with each other and talked about how difficult it is to deal with the feelings and dilemmas – the relief at not being there in the middle of it all and the guilt of not being part of it, involved. We had run away from it, left the suffering and struggle to others. We preferred to be in comfort, safe. She said, 'When I talk to my English friends, they say things like "What would you have done if you were there?" "But that's not the point," I say.' 'Yes,' I agreed, 'that's not the point.' They don't understand, you see. They have nothing in their experience to relate it to, to compare it with.

I remembered how, during the Revolution, I had longed to be

in Iran, to be involved. And I remembered how, soon after the Revolution, when I first heard that four women had been stoned to death in Iran for supposedly immoral activities, prostitution, that night all of my insides ached, as if I felt part of their pain. They were a part of me, we had the same roots. We were born and brought up in the same country, same culture. We breathed the same air, read the same literature, the same poetry ...

I remembered the day I went to the hospital to meet the brother of a friend who had been shot during the Revolution. He was paralysed from the waist down. I felt like hugging him and saying, 'I know what you have been through. Part of it is for me too. You have taken on my struggle as well. You have paid heavily, and many others too. I ran away, didn't I? Part of your loss is mine, part of your pain is mine.'

We talked about the similarities between Iran and South Africa. I remembered that book, *Cry the Beloved Country*, by Alan Paton, a South African writer. When I read it I thought how close it was in some ways to the Iranian situation. I felt particularly touchy about this issue, I suppose because of my writing. I am touching my roots, old wounds are being opened up.

The next day, waiting for a train at Wandsworth Station, I cast my mind back over the previous day's events in the class and how I was touched. I remembered when I met my husband and he took me out for the first time. In the restaurant he said, 'I'll sit here, next to you. No good sitting opposite. You need me close to you.' That touched me. It drew me close to him. On another occasion he said he liked sitting on the floor. I was touched. The floor, the ground, meant a lot to me. It echoed my childhood experience of the floor and of the ground.

In the little village in Iran where I grew up we sat on the floor, slept on the floor, ate on the floor, worked on the floor. I remembered my little wooden hand-spinner. When I spun wool with it, it went round and round, with one twist of the spindle on the floor, so steady. The sound of it, the feel of it, the result of it was magic. The floor, the ground, gave me a sense of steadiness, firmness, continuity. It was reliable, always there, hard, crude, patient.

Women gave birth on the floor. My mother, as each contraction came, would go out into the yard and lay herself, on all fours, on the big stone slab in the corner of the yard, which served as a shelf usually. It was a symbol of strength. She hugged that stone and it was as though the slab took on the strength of the contraction. When it stopped, she went indoors to continue her housework.

That morning, the ticket collector at the station touched me on the shoulder as though saying, 'There, that's because you can't see the tenderness in my face.' It all happens in a flash. That's the beauty of it. It's not the result of thought. It happens spontaneously. And that gives the touching quality to it.

My two-year-old son wants me to draw a train for him. I do my best. 'But it has no wheels, mummy,' he protests. I try to put wheels on for him. 'Here it is, I've done it,' I say, feeling awkward, unsure. 'That's not wheels,' he screams. Tears the paper in a rage. Goes away from me, sobbing. No one else would do to put the wheels on the train. He wants me, his mother, to put the wheels on.

Now he is three. This morning I can't find his shoes anywhere. It is getting late for nursery. 'Please, darling, will you help mummy to find your shoes?' 'No, if you can't see, I can't see,' he says laughingly. It hurts. I have to bear his pain as well as mine. And later, 'I put my bike right there in the middle, you will fall over it, you can't see, ha ha ha.'

As he started school, he became more aware of my foreign origin. 'You go back to Iran where you've come from, mummy. We don't want you here,' he said when he was cross. 'I'll tell Uncle Akbar to take you back to Iran.' 'I am English,' he would say, with pride in his voice. He wants me to be like other mothers in his school, sighted, English. To him I am very different. This is uncomfortable, very uncomfortable at times. He hates my white stick. 'Please, mummy, when you come to fetch me from school, don't bring your stick, hide it away. Give it to me, I will break it. You embarrass me, mummy. People stare at you. I don't want to walk with you.'

On one occasion he said in a rage, 'You can't even see, can you?' 'Can you?' he repeated forcefully. I felt like screaming at the top of my voice and saying, 'It's not my fault, you wretched child, how can you be so cruel?' But the screams are squashed in my throat, which feels like splitting any second. I have to bear his pain and mine. He is only expressing in words his anger at my blindness. He is not hitting me as he used to when he was younger. So I reply, simply, 'No.' My voice is unfamiliar, shaky. I am defenceless, vulnerable, like a baby. I can't protest. But I take comfort in the fact that he feels safe enough with me to express his feelings of anger and frustration at my blindness and foreignness.

Although his occasional outbursts cause me enormous pain and distress, my consolation is, if he is able to express this frustration now, trusting me so much that I won't crumble away, that his anger won't destroy me, then hopefully in the future he will be a freer individual and we will have a healthier relationship together.

He trusts me with his secrets. I think he tells me everything. 'Don't tell this to daddy, mummy.' Or the teacher, or the mother of a friend.

I used to touch people easily and freely. If I was talking about something exciting I might touch the person next to me and say, 'Do you know what happened this morning?' When I first came to England I formed a friendship with Carol, a psychology student. When I touched her I noticed that she drew back, and then one day she said, 'I must tell you something, Gohar. In this country we don't touch amongst the same sex, otherwise people might think we are homosexuals.' That inhibited me from touching my own sex. My Eastern culture had already prohibited me from touching the opposite sex. What do I do then? Ignore people's physical being?

Some time later I made friends with a Palestinian girl. One day I was waiting for her at the bus stop. Suddenly I heard her calling my name and running towards me. She hugged and kissed me heartily. I just froze, could not respond. I had lost my ability, the spontaneity, to touch.

One day in my adult education massage class, when we were practising, I was struck by the individuality of the face of the woman I was massaging. I had forgotten how people's faces differ, because in my day-to-day contact I seldom touch their faces. It would be nice if I could touch people's faces, I thought. But what is it that stops me? Inhibition? This society disapproves of touching. I am told people look strangely at us when I walk arm in arm with a girlfriend, until they notice that I cannot see. My blindness legitimises my being touched.

My son, when he was three years old and describing wallpaper in a friend's house, said longingly, 'Mummy, I wish you could see.' I felt the pain in his voice. 'Yes, darling,' I replied in surprise. It touches me in the heart and I feel helpless.

He went through a phase of trying desperately to make his drawings tactile to me. He would sit for hours experimenting, struggling to find a way. He got the special pen that I write braille with and other sharp instruments, like a nail, a needle and the like, anything he could find, to raise his drawings. He would go on for hours. Ideas would bubble out of his little head. 'Mummy, what if . . . ? Come and see this one, feel this one.' Again, I felt helpless, unable to assist him to find a solution. It hurt both of us. My five-year-old seemed like a creative scientist, trying in desperation to find a solution to a major problem. We both felt hurt, disappointed, as though we had failed.

Some touches repel. 'I know all about the blind. My aunt was blind,' the woman at the bus stop says, when I ask her to tell me when my bus arrives. Or 'There's a good boy, you're mummy's eyes, aren't you? Look after her,' from the man in the street, when offering to help us cross the road. It makes me furious. I feel like hitting him and saying, 'Don't you *dare* make him feel responsible for me. I didn't have him to be my eyes!' Often I can't think of anything to say. My anger and embarrassment in front of my son crush me and I remain speechless.

I used to touch children freely, cuddle them, as I had in Iran, until some mothers told me their children didn't like to be touched. Now I hesitate before touching a child. It maddens me because I was brought up to touch and to be touched all the time. At night, in the village, we slept together as a family. A Pakistani friend, a young woman, when she returned from a visit to Pakistan, told me that one night all the cousins and close friends decided they would sleep together, just as in the old days. So ten or twelve of them grabbed anything they could find, a quilt or something similar, to put on the floor to make one big bed, and all of them, of all ages, including some boys of fourteen and fifteen, all slept in a row.

I used to touch my son all the time, cuddle him, bathe him, dress him. He would sit on my lap to watch television or to play a game together. 'Come, mummy, I want to sit on your lap,' he would demand. And I loved that. But once he started school he gradually moved away from me. Now, our physical contact has become much less. This makes me sad. For me, touch was a substitute for seeing him, and now it is diminishing. It is as though he is moving out of focus to me. When someone tells me 'Your son is beautiful. Do you know what beautiful eyes he has?', I think 'No, I don't. How can I?' The pain is excruciating. I envy those who can see his eyes. It makes me cross. Everyone else can see him but me. When I say 'Give mummy a cuddle', he refuses. It feels as though I am losing him, a part of him, or that I am losing a lot of what I could have, what I had. Loss. It hurts.

My earliest memory of my father is of sitting on his lap as he feeds me grated carrot and speaks lovingly to me – 'My angel, my sweetheart,' he calls me. I can't remember his face, but I remember the warmth of his body, the sweetness of his voice, the taste of the carrot. My memory is of feelings and the sense of touch. I don't remember his face, even though this was before I lost my sight.

Touch can be so beautiful to me. Sometimes my son is cruel. But at other times he flings his arms around me and kisses me on the eyes and says, 'Mummy, I love you, you are the best mummy in the world.' His touch, the tenderness, lift me right above the clouds, into the sunlight. They warm me right through and I just float, and I forget all the troubles of the world, and all the suffering is worth it for these moments.

Aspen

Our Friendship Is Mellowed to a Whisper, Sister

Living so far apart
I relied on you to tell me
what was going on for you.
You told me nothing:
afraid of complaining
you said your disability
was a small part of you.

When I deteriorated myself
I couldn't talk about it
because you might think
that was giving in, or
making it too important.

What's happened to our closeness?
That valuable, precious
lovegift?
Starved in the dark
gnawed by doubt, it's
too brittle now
to pick up.

Being political about disability
has given me teeth
to eat it.

Maria Jastrzębska

Friends

1

thank god
for the small procession of friends
who knock on my door
bringing me flowers and newspaper cuttings
interesting books
or the wrong kind of apples
because I've forgotten to explain
which ones I like

friends who take the initiative
in supermarkets or at the grocer's
adding things to my list
forcing me to treat myself
to unexpected strawberries
or mango
friends who send me cards
from abroad
friends who go on believing
in my recovery

2

they seem
like circus dancers
daring and fast
everything they wear is brightly coloured
when they talk about their lives

I imagine them
somersaulting through the air
hanging by a silver thread
from the high wire

I think:
that's what I must have been doing
till I fell
landed in this bed again
caught in the tangled nets
of illness
telling myself it could be worse

3

when they talk
the noise grazes my senses
so I know my body will tremble
for a long time
after they've gone

other times
they're the ones
who seem tired
they seem to find relief
in this quiet room
they move
into the huge, uncluttered spaces
in my diary and like it there
they can relax
knowing there's no need
to perform

4

and then there's the ones
who say: *I wouldn't mind being ill
just a little
– oh not like you of course –*

but I can't afford to
as though this illness was a luxury
I can't stop
who else would take over
the kids, my job
who indeed?

as if they envied
this curtain
that comes down
so indiscriminately
that gets me out
of whatever it is
I never really wanted to do
and in the same sudden gesture
cuts me off
from all the things
I long to do
this stillness
after the curtain's come down
this is how tired women
without a moment to themselves
define luxury

.

Diane Pungartnik

One More Time: A Horror Story

I was eighteen. I was dressed for school and about to have breakfast with my sister. The next thing I knew, I was in a hospital being looked at by a doctor.

I was twenty-two. I got up early to go to the radio station for a show I helped to produce. I was dressed and ready to go. A while later I was still dressed and ready to go, but a lot had happened in the meantime. That time they put me on 300 milligrams of phenytoin daily.

Many successful, drug-taking years later a friend said to me, 'Wouldn't it be better to have a seizure from time to time, rather than taking all those pills?' 'No,' I replied.

I was twenty-nine. It was very late at night and I was having a little something to eat before going to bed. The next thing I knew, the cup of tea was spilled on the sofa and the shreddies were all over me. I looked stupidly about me, walked over to the table where my diary was and stared at the page for that day, mentally going over everything I'd done since the morning.

'Oh,' I thought slowly, 'I've done it again.'

The next day things were not too clear, but I went to the theatre where I was performing at lunchtime and got through the play with no trouble, though I couldn't remember what I did afterwards. The run of the show ended five days later and then I could collapse.

I wasn't too bad in the morning because nothing happened to upset me, but by two o'clock in the afternoon I was shattered physically and had a migraine. I knew from experience that I wouldn't be completely recovered for three months.

How do you explain to your doctor that you need a sick certificate for a month (and may need it for much longer), when all the people with epilepsy she's heard about have frequent seizures and sleep them off in a day?

How do you get through to the people at the DSS and the housing office when there are delays for no reason and you have to wait for hours and you're so tired and the least thing makes you cry?

What do you say to the man at Social Services who turns you down for a bus pass and obviously thinks you're taking advantage of the system?

And, my God, what do you say to the senior registrar at the Royal Hospital for Nervous Diseases, who is completely uninterested in your case and tells you you should be grateful since there are people worse off than you?

I didn't say anything to any of them. I begged them for what I needed and when I met with resistance I didn't fight; I didn't have the strength. Instead I cried. I cried on the steps of the Social Security building. I cried in the waiting room at the housing office. I cried in the waiting room at the hospital. I cried at the bus stop.

I didn't cry in front of my friends. They took one look at my death's head face and saw all they needed to know. The one who had thought I should stop taking my pills retracted her suggestion.

Many more successful, drug-taking years have passed. If I'm out late and a friend offers to put me up for the night, I say no, I've got to go home and take my pills. I'm very lucky to have a drug that works and I'm more *grateful* for it than that doctor could ever comprehend, but I know I could have a seizure any day, for no particular reason.

And when I have the next one, I fervently hope that the social services, the benefits offices and the hospitals and health centres are fully staffed with disabled employees. Then I can go in and know that I will be received with understanding. May it come speedily and in our days.

Diane Kenyon

Reaction-Interaction

Most hearing people perceive deafness as a medical problem to be cured, but the pill has their name on it!

Such a little pill, compounded of improved communication skills, attitudes and knowledge, a dose of visual awareness and a sprinkling of sensitivity and confidence.

I smile as I begin my daily patter. 'Could you speak more slowly please, and move your lips, as I am deaf. This will help me to understand what you are saying.' This smile is not conjured up to sell my deafness. I am a naturally cheerful person, I have a confident approach to my disability.

I am deadly serious about my directive. I expect people to listen to my request and try to comply. This is the only stance that I can take if we are to communicate on the level that comes after *'Pleased to meet you'*. If we cannot negotiate a channel whereby our minds can make contact, then these people simply move on, deftly passing me by in some socially acceptable way. For me, there is no one to move on to.

Speech sounds are meant to be heard with ears, not seen by eyes. Yet eyes to *hear with* are what deaf people have.

Whenever I jar up against another human being, it is useless just to tell them that I am deaf. I have to hunt for ways of explaining that their method of communication thrusts me into isolation. Although my body and its clothing are in the room of life, I the person am not. My participation is stunted by their immobile lips, hands and attitudes.

I see myself as a warm person, human contact is life to me. I am always working to assure people that I understand their difficulties in adapting their mode of verbal communication to give me access. I am an optimist, I always hope that when we meet next, they will *remember* my needs. Usually they have forgotten. I don't want to be thought of as a nuisance. I don't want always to prompt and remind.

Reactions to my declaration of deafness are verbal, so once again I am disadvantaged. Using my hearing aids and much guesswork, I strain to understand their handicapping responses.

I give a talk at a lunch club. The first man I mention my deafness to, cups his hand behind his ear, saying, 'What? What?'

A mousetrap kind of reaction to cover his embarrassment. He does not mean to be offensive, his behaviour is that of an elephant who stands on your foot, totally unconscious of the effect.

Another man, with enormous relish, relates a joke about hearing aids.

He delivers the lines with the confidence of the totally ignorant, expecting it to give as much pleasure to me as to the assembled others. I do not know that he is telling a joke, let alone a joke about deafness. Later a friend tells me. It feels as if someone is speaking about me in a foreign language, laughingly telling a group of strangers something very private.

My stoical front temporarily recedes and, needing a bit of empathy, I share a couple of moans about deafness.

'Yes, Diane, but we all have our problems', delivered with a finger-wagging, reprimanding look suggesting that I am caught up too much with my disability. All my efforts to constantly and anxiously balance the problems and distractions that people have with my own communication needs, get me nowhere.

'I'm no good at all this "mouthing" lark', referring to speaking clearly.

A statement which cleanly slices through any link between us. No 'But how can I improve?', no meeting me halfway.

Someone thrashes their hands at me and asks, 'Do you do all this stuff then?" meaning signing/fingerspelling.

THIS STUFF? It's my ramp, my wide door entry to human

culture. This stuff! Illuminating fingers forming alphabet letters that make sense of mouth movements.

'*My cousin was deaf, no problems at all. She could understand me fine.*'

Pressed further it is revealed that this paragon had only the edge off her hearing, and 'understanding' meant nodding her head at all times.

'*Isn't the deaf* MP *wonderful, he manages so well, doesn't he?*'

I must bear up, be undemanding and accept my lot.

'*Can't they operate?*'

Then I can be cured and they won't have to be perturbed by me.

'*Ah, but you heard me when I offered you a gin and tonic, didn't you?*'

You only hear when you want to. Likewise 'My grandfather was deaf, put it on though.'

'*Can she understand me?*'

To a friend, turning immediately away from me. Sometimes in the form of nervous half laughs, along with 'What do I do now?'

'*No problem, no problem, I've worked with the deaf. I'm used to such people.*' *Shouted at me through rigid lips eclipsed by a tatty moustache.*

An 'on the ball, I've got it taped' kind of attitude.

'*Is your daughter with you? I could speak to her instead.*'

From people who panic at my first 'Pardon?'

Silence whilst they fight for composure, followed by a politely distancing comment.

I can't retaliate because I can't hear it!

The deafness which alienates and dehumanises is caused by inaccessible words. To be denied access to language which takes liberties with you is an assault on your control over your life. The human contact deaf people need is what causes us the greatest unhappiness.

It feels good to be with other deaf people and have relaxed and fluent conversation. But I live in this world and, like anyone else, I want access to the widest spectrum of human life. I am determined to achieve this for myself, and the new generation of deaf people.

Dorothy Miles

To a Deaf Child

You hold the word in hand;
and though your voice may speak, never
(though you might tutor it for ever)
can it achieve the hand-wrought eloquence
of this sign. Who in the word alone can say
that day is sunlight, night is dark?
                    Oh, remark
the signs for living, for being
inspired, excited – how similar they.

Your lightest word in hand
lifts like a butterfly, or folds
in liquid motion: each gesture holds
echoes of action or shape or reasoning.
Within your hands perhaps you form a clear
new vision – Man's design for living:
                    so giving
sign-ificance to Babel's tongues
that henceforth he who sees aright may hear.

You hold the word in hand
and offer the palm of friendship;
at frontiers where men of speech lend lip-
service to brotherhood, you pass, unhampered
by sounds that drown the meaning, or by fear
of the foreign-word-locked fetter;

oh, better
the word in hand than a thousand
spilled from the mouth upon the hearless ear.

Millee Hill

Patricia's Mother

I was so excited at the prospect of returning home that I could barely contain myself. I wanted to leap from my seat and rush into the cockpit, wrestle the controls from the pilot and guide the plane home, faster, much faster.

'Oh don't be silly.' I laughed at my own thought. 'You can't leap from your seat and you most certainly couldn't fly a plane.' I had long accepted the fact that I would never walk again, but perhaps I could add one more item to my long list of things to do, learn to fly a plane.

As I gazed out of the window, glorying in the sensation of flying and of seeing the clouds below instead of above me, a feeling of fear and apprehension slowly started to creep over me. I was born in Bermuda, but, having spent many years in America, Canada and other countries, I was accustomed to flying back and forth across the Atlantic. I had always enjoyed flying – it wasn't *that* which was terrifying me. That I was going home to my beloved island could not be the reason I was increasingly filled with dread.

I was eagerly looking forward to the spiritual comfort of the jewel-blue sky with her ice-cream clouds ruled by the hot Bermuda sun; the cool cobalt-and-green sea embroidered with her salmony pink sandy beaches; the wonderful magic of the haughty Palmetto and Casarina trees. I especially love my island in the summertime: the brown-skinned Bermudians lazing in the sun, drinking beer and eating oysters; the long smouldering summer evenings full of the wafting smells of barbecues and charged with the rumpt-te-tum-tum of reggae, calypso and soul music. I yearned to get caught up in the thick of it all. So it wasn't the thought of returning home which was scaring me.

What was petrifying me was the thought of returning home, not as the skinny, long-legged Millee who used to run so fast and jump so high that people used to joke 'You'd think she was training for the Olympics'; not as the Millee who used to swim like a fish and who, on a good day, could hold her breath under water for longer than all but one or two of the gang; not as the Millee who used to walk or cycle for miles along the beach and the track; not as the Millee who used to dance like Michael Jackson and Bobby Brown (well, James Brown, then). No, it wasn't the thought of returning home that was frightening me. It was the thought of arriving home, not as the runner, the dancer, the cyclist, but as Millee the wheelchair-user!

I was returning home a different person – a disabled person – and I was frightened. Frightened of how I would be received by my family and friends, who I'd not seen for years. Frightened at how they would react and how I would cope. Frightened about where I would live and if I would work. Frightened about everything and everyone. Simply frightened!

Over time that fear was to evaporate. I cannot pinpoint the day, the moment in time when I stopped being afraid. There was no sudden awakening, no startling awareness, no catastrophic event which frightened the fear out of me, no catalyst, even, which fostered others' acceptance of me. I only know that my family and friends gradually became used to me, and I slowly stopped being afraid. Although I was no longer that all-singing, all-dancing Millee, the new Millee no longer caused instant whispers, furtive glances and feeble excuses to allow for escape.

In fact, people became so accustomed to me that they even started taking me around my old neighbourhood stomping ground. It was often eerie to wheel over the places where I once had walked. To look up at the trees which I once had climbed, unable to reach the branches where I once had sat; eerie to be barred from the places where I once ran free because my wheelchair could not traverse the jagged rocks which embraced the land along the North and South shores.

One of my favourite spots was 'the Jungle', as we used to call it as children. A small patch of trees and bushes with dense undergrowth heavily intertwined with wild berries and fruit trees, about two hundred yards behind my high school. I would wander around the outer perimeter, my wheelchair unable to penetrate the inner reaches where I once used to spend the odd day playing 'hookey' from school.

I remembered how we used to get such a kick out of being so close to school, yet able to 'run wild' all day without getting caught. My most vivid memory of the Jungle, however, was of the one day that I did get caught. I had spent the entire morning away from classes roaming the bush and stuffing myself full of the not-quite-ripe loquats. By early afternoon I was so ill that one of my fellow miscreants had to go and call a teacher to drive me home. I soon recovered from my upset stomach but spent the next few days in mortal fear of my mother's wrath and visits from the truant officer.

On other days I was taken down the hill behind my house to 'the Rocks' – the tall majestic purple-blue-grey cliffs off which I used to dive into the sea. I'd swim for yards under the surface until I was completely out of breath, when I would rush to the surface gasping for air. Then, on one fateful day, I was jostled off the cliff and tumbled into the water offside, snapping my spine irrevocably in two.

I particularly loved going into the city to shop. It took a certain knack to wend my wheelchair down the narrow aisles of the tiny local shops and I always went in fear and trepidation of knocking some expensive item off the shelf and breaking it. Shopping at home always put me in mind of a popular local song entitled 'Bermuda Is Another World'. The little shops on the island were just about as far removed from the megastores and hypermarkets I was obliged to shop at in America and Canada as one could get.

I had a compulsion to buy anything distinctively Bermudian,

whether I needed it or not. Bermuda shorts, which I never wore; books about the island which were written for tourists; hand-made sandals crafted by delinquent boys on the work farm; locally produced perfumes and homegrown spices; huge bottles of Bermuda black rum, and anything, simply anything, carved from Bermuda Cedar trees. I would strategically place these treasured items about my cold Toronto flat in a vain attempt to make it feel like my warm Bermuda home.

But my favourite activity that 'first' summer turned out to be just sitting beside the road watching for that van to pass. The road was about one hundred and fifty yards away from my house and since the day I saw him, I would employ any manner of means or invent any excuse in order to solicit someone's help to push me over the gravelly, unpaved path to the side of the street. And there I would sit – sometimes for hours – waiting for that van to pass with him in it.

The first day that I saw him drive by, I was waiting beside the road for my transport to come. As he passed, he smiled a wide smile. He was certainly not the Adonis of my dreams, but after that smile, I had no inclination to go into work at my part-time, voluntary, boring job. I returned home and allowed myself to be carried away by daydreams.

In Bermuda, everybody seems to know everybody else. What's more, everybody seems to know everybody else's business. So it didn't take me long to learn that he was the manager of a group of stores and would commute between branches along the North Shore Road which passed in front of my house.

Thus started my regular pilgrimages, at least two or three times a week, out to the side of the street. There I would wait and wait, in the boiling sun, often without shade and soaked to the skin with sweat – itchy, uncomfortable and dying of thirst, just to catch a glimpse of that passing smile and the briefest of waves. He never stopped to speak or linger, but I didn't care, I just needed to see him. Only after seeing him did I feel like flagging down a car and going into work. But more often I would get one of the children who were always hanging around to push me home, or to turn and get one of my family to do it.

Then I would sit on my back porch, look out at the ocean and dream wonderful dreams.

As it was summertime, there were always lots of kids playing in the open space between the road and my house. Dirt cricket, marbles, tops, jacks, hopscotch, skipping rope, tag – anything and everything and often two or three games at a time. It didn't take them long to cotton on to the fact that I paid them not the slightest mind until after that white van had passed. Only then did I 'poke my nose' into their play with score keeping, shouts of encouragement, instructions, advice, or just plain bossing about. My trips into work became less and less frequent. Sitting beside the road became far more important.

Soon the children had another game to play as they began to tease me with a little rhyme one of them had made up.

'Miss Hill's in love with the man in the van.
She comes to see him whenever she can'

they would sing mockingly, circling ever closer to me, trying to provoke a reaction, while I did my best to ignore them.

'Miss Hill's in love with the man in the van,' they would chant up in my face, then laugh and skip away. I hated being teased and hated even more being called Miss Hill. That was what they called my mother and I wasn't that old. However, I rarely challenged them, fearing he might go past the moment I turned away to have a go.

As he was not unknown to my family, I plotted and schemed and was soon able to insinuate myself into social situations where I knew I would see him. Very quickly a flirtatious relationship developed between us. As I pondered how to get on to phase three, I continued my treks out to the roadside. I was left in no doubt that he was interested, as he smiled much more broadly and began to drive by perceptibly more slowly. He also took to going fishing with my brothers which would bring him to the beach where I sunbathed, or into my house for a cool drink or evening meal. 'Ah,' I thought, 'phase three, we're on our way.'

By this time the teasing had become incessant and the taunting, chanting, giggling brats had added another verse to their little song:

'Miss Hill's in love with the man in the van.
She comes to see him whenever she can.
And when she can't she stays at home
And the man in the van drives by like stone.'

One day as I sat waiting, Patricia, one of my tormentors, came up to me in floods of tears. In between her gasps for breath, she managed to splutter, 'My mama said I should come and say sorry for making fun of you.' Having barely finished her watery sentence and without waiting for me to accept her apology, she sped off in the direction of her house, from where, I noticed, her mother was approaching. As she went past, Patricia gave a wide berth to this big, overbearing woman, obviously to avoid another slap.

The large, formidable figure moved towards me like a rolling storm cloud. A dark-skinned woman in a brightly coloured floral dress, barefooted and headscarved, she had hands like a stevedore which she had placed firmly on her ample hips. As the sun set on those summer evenings which left the sky with a dusky orange glow, I had often heard her calling in Patricia and James, and I knew that she had a voice to rival a thunderclap.

She loomed over me, hands on hips, dusty feet apart, her huge frame blocking out the sun. I anticipated treatment similar to that meted out to Patricia, so when she opened her mouth to speak I flinched. However, instead of the earth-shattering noise I expected, her voice was surprisingly soft. But her words doused me like ice-cold rainwater.

'I don't want to worry you mother about this,' she began. (In Bermuda, when a neighbour sees what they deem to be inappropriate behaviour in a 'child', it is customary for them to approach the child's parents in order for them to correct the offending behaviour. For some reason, in my case this neighbour felt it entirely appropriate to approach me directly.)

'God knows, Madelyn's got enough to worry about with you,' she continued. 'But really, love, don't you realise that you are making a fool of yourself, wasting your time sitting here every day all day waiting to see that boy? Don't you know that being the way you are no man will ever want you? You'll never have a boyfriend, love, and no man will want to marry you. Besides which,' she added, 'people like you can't have babies. I'm only telling you this for your own good, love, so you won't get hurt.'

She ranted on for quite some time but I didn't hear her last few sentences – which was just as well, as I was too flabbergasted to make a response. I don't even rightly remember her leaving. What I do remember is that I did not see him that day, though I know for sure that he drove past. I stayed there for a good long while, unable even to summon enough energy to call one of the kids.

I didn't go out to the road again, and on the days that he came to the house I stayed in my room. At the end of my summer vacation I returned to Canada without seeing him again. Some time after I had left the island, I received a letter from him which I kept for a long time before I destroyed it, unopened. Patricia's mother's words were to live with me for many, many years.

PART FOUR

Maria Jastrzębska

The Horns of My Dilemma

I seem to spend
Half my time
Wishing
I had horns
On my head
To look the part
A rarity
Like the almost extinct
Wild bison of eastern Poland.
So children could stop and point
Look mummy that lady's got horns!
Before being hurried along
By some embarrassed adult.
Horns or else flickering antennae
Which bleeped
Unmistakably alien
Or extra-terrestrial
Hooves which sent showers
Of sparks flying
Whenever they touched the ground.
Devilish, wicked, supernatural.
And a tail,
Oh yes a tail
Swishing and bushy
With fronds and tassles
In luminous green, I think.
So nobody could make the usual assumptions,

So I wouldn't have to explain
How I'm different
We'd get this fact established
Right away
Because what hurts worse
Than any pain
Is the denial.

The trouble is
I spend just as much time
Trying to explain
With increasing impatience
That in fact
I don't have horns
Or hooves,
Not even a bushy tail.

Trying not to frighten
People away
Reassuring anxious relatives
And friends.

Some things I play down
Others I censor right out
Working overtime
To bridge a widening gap.
Searching for common ground.
So as not to be labelled
Into oblivion
So I'm not written off
Before I've even had a chance.

Here are my tears, I say
Salty and wet like yours
Here are my hopes
Which need tending
Like anything you want to grow

And what hurts worse
Than any pain
Is the denial.

Why is it people
Either think I'm just like them
Or else
Like nothing on this earth
And no part of their lives?

If I can live with this dilemma
It doesn't seem too much
To ask others
To recognise
How I'm different
But very ordinary
Ordinary and very different.

Sally French

Equal Opportunities... Yes, Please

In 1967, I enrolled in my local further education college for a one-year GCE O level course. The college had never taken a visually impaired student before but after much deliberation and anxious discussion they decided to accept me provided I could manage without any extra help or support.

This turned out to be one of the most positive learning experiences of my life. My 'special school' had done very little to encourage my academic side and I was determined to succeed. Despite the harsh conditions attached, their attitude was easy to cope with because it was, at least, honest and direct. It was not unusual for staff to congratulate me for managing as well as the fully sighted students! The rhetoric of equal opportunities policies had not yet touched this institution and there were no attempts to make me 'just like everyone else'. There were of course pressures to minimise my disability, not to rock the boat, but no one pretended that I was *equal* or that I could be made *normal*.

Despite their pronouncements that no one would assist me, many staff proved eager to help on an individual basis. The English teacher wrote all her comments with a thick black pen so that I could read them, the biology teacher gave me duplicate diagrams of those she drew on the blackboard and the history teacher, whose enthusiasm for the subject would have made anyone's lack of access entirely intolerable to him, abandoned visual aids altogether. Extra time was arranged in the examinations and my papers were enlarged and printed on white paper rather than beige, with the minimum of fuss. My self-esteem began to grow, I felt relaxed and valued.

Not everyone was helpful, but the modest assistance I was given then was greater than anything I have since received despite all the guidelines and policy documents which have been produced in the name of Equal Opportunities.

For more than twenty years I have studied and worked in educational institutions. My experience as a disabled woman has led me to believe that equal opportunities policies in such places offer, at best, tokenist help such as a piece of equipment, but also allow for enormous complacency and hypocrisy. There is a lot of pressure on employers to be seen to be 'doing something' but the 'solutions' adopted often take no account of the individual needs of disabled people.

A visually impaired person may, for example, be given a special piece of equipment like a computer. This may enable them to do the job but also has the effect of others assuming that all the problems are now solved. The computer was very expensive so this person must now be *equal* and they must be *normal*. They must ask for nothing more. Technology is often used as a substitute for human help, although for many disabled people it is the quick and flexible assistance of colleagues which is most useful. We are not supposed to query the benefits of such technology or to suggest that, however much it cost, there are still difficulties for us at work.

I had a very hard time at work when I said that I could not see sufficiently to use the on-site computers. With a lot of aggression and resentment, I was told that a blind colleague had not had any of these problems. There was no recognition of our differing impairments, working methods, or roles within the organisation. It seemed to be assumed that I was using my disability as a tactic to avoid work. I still don't know how to resolve the intense anger I feel about this.

The advantages of technological solutions to non-disabled people are that they look more impressive, usually cost less and don't interfere with their lives. Electronic 'talking signposts' are at this moment being considered for installation in the grounds of the university where I work, because, it is said, they will assist visually impaired people to find their way around. They are triggered by a hand-held transmitter and it was proposed that a spare transmitter should be made available for visitors until I pointed out that this would be extraordinarily unhelpful and unfriendly, especially as even sighted visitors are often escorted round the grounds!

These signposts might satisfy the creative talents of their inventors, they certainly don't satisfy my needs. What I need, of course, are pavements and corridors which are free of obstacles, and people with the time and patience to show me around (and to do so more than once). Twenty years ago, before equal opportunities were thought of, I found this happened automatically, but lately it has stopped. Perhaps the arguments about the rights of disabled people have made others nervous of offering help. Perhaps it is because the organisations I have worked in have become larger and more impersonal. I don't know.

Administrators seem unwilling to understand how different the needs of visually impaired people can be. Large print is a case in point. Some visually impaired people find it very useful but for others it reduces their visual field to a word or even part of a word and for them, the density, colour and style of print may be more important. When I try to discuss these issues with my colleagues I can feel them switching off. I am constantly asking people to write clearly or not to give me microprint but, even if they comply, they rarely do so more than once. If I reject their 'help' or ask for some change, I sometimes feel that I am seen as ungrateful and unfriendly.

A real interest for committees involved in developing equal opportunities policies is monitoring how interviews are conducted and this is fine as far as it goes, but there is not enough concern about how disabled people will manage once they are in the organisation. People are so nervous about interviewing us and so keen not to be thought prejudiced that there can be a lot of dishonesty. I was certainly misled at my last job interview.

Everyone seemed to be trying so hard to be 'positive' about

my impairment that it was barely mentioned and for once I was spared all those awkward and sceptical questions about how I could possibly manage the job with my degree of sight. I usually like to discuss my disability on my own terms to ensure that I can cope with the work without too much stress, but on this occasion I felt inhibited. The fact that they had invited me to apply and seemed to be welcoming me as a disabled person lulled me into a false sense of security and this led me to make a less than informed decision.

The problems started when I accepted the job. I was asked to travel all over the country to places I had never been. I had to find particular houses in specific roads, which was difficult and stressful. I also discovered that I needed to transfer to a different computer system whose software was grossly incompatible with the magnification software I require. I am not computer-minded but was forced to resolve all kinds of hideous problems myself as the computer department flatly refused to have anything to do with me. I had no access to the extensive computer training facilities enjoyed by my non-disabled colleagues although I did manage to squeeze enough money out of my department to finance a few days of individual tuition which I organised myself.

There was nothing in the structure of the organisation to accommodate me. I found myself trying to read microscopic print, print on a coloured background and appalling handwriting, or attempting to take part in meetings and seminars where none of the information was presented in an accessible format.

For the first time in twenty years of work, I could not see to read the numbers on the doors as they were very high and small. The only way of finding out where I had to go was to knock on the nearest office door and ask for help. This frequently resulted in the embarrassment of interrupting meetings and interviews or else there was no one there to ask. All of this left me feeling helpless, angry and very 'disabled'.

Another vital issue for me is time. Equal opportunities policies never tackle this issue, even though it is so crucial to visually impaired and other disabled people. A blind colleague who has all the special equipment on offer told me that he works sixty hours a week in order to hold down his job. Imagine the outcry if any other group of people worked almost twice as long as their colleagues for no extra reward! My job involves a lot of reading and my reading speed is slow. I have never calculated the exact hours I work. Perhaps if I did I would have to acknowledge how little time there is left for me beyond my employment.

Equal opportunity policies for disabled people, where they exist, often go no deeper than the idea of saying that they should employ more of us. Once they get a disabled person in the building it is convenient and cheap for employers to believe that we want to be treated 'just like anyone else'. A friend of mine who queried the delay of a vital piece of equipment was told by her disdainful manager 'I have worked with many blind people and they all wanted to be treated normally'.

The employers of disabled people need to acknowledge that along with the skills for which we have been employed we may also have particular needs and requirements and it is the responsibility of the employer to meet these needs. That is what equal opportunities practice should mean. My own attempts at work to collude with the expectations that I should be just like everyone else mean that I always try to minimise the difficulties I face at work. I do it to get the work I want but in doing so I have to deny who I really am.

When I have received recognition regarding my needs at work, this has sometimes been seen by the giver as a charitable act for which I should be grateful and beholden. I cannot see to read or write if the sun shines on my page, yet in one job I had to fight to get a curtain put up at my window. I was frequently reminded of the cost and once it was up, people didn't seem to be able to pass my desk without enquiring whether I was pleased with it or telling me how great it was that I'd got it. I was being given two distinct messages; first, that I had been granted a very special 'favour' and second, that I must ask for nothing more.

Expressing gratitude for a kind or thoughtful act is something I do willingly. Expressing gratitude when I receive what should be my right is a dangerous move. A colleague recently attended a degree ceremony as a spectator and later wrote to complain about the inaccessibility for some disabled graduates. The reply she received was short and curt with no apology. Enclosed were photocopies of letters from four disabled students expressing their extreme gratitude for attending the ceremony at all. If we expect little, we get nothing.

In these more enlightened days, I am often asked to educate everyone else on all matters relating to disability. 'We know nothing about it, you must teach us,' they say. This may be progress but I don't know 'all about it' and, although I have a clear perspective on what should be the rights of disabled people at work, I am not an expert on the individual needs of other disabled colleagues. No formal structures have been developed in which this process of educating my colleagues can take place and sometimes it feels that, although I am asked endless questions about disability, I am rarely taken seriously and what I do say is forgotten or ignored.

I am becoming increasingly wary of involvement in discussions which are stressful and make me feel that I am viewed by others as a problem, but which do not change anything. If organisations were really committed to understanding disability they would put as much thought and resources into acquiring the necessary knowledge and skills as they do into numerous other matters deemed to be important. Continually arguing and campaigning for our rights as lone disabled people with little or no support from others is exhausting. The fear of being labelled 'difficult', with all the implications for references and promotion in the very competitive academic world, leads many disabled people, myself included, to remain passive. I am not happy working like this but sometimes I am too tired and too frustrated to be any different.

I am on the Equal Opportunities Committee at work but I do not know what equal opportunities means. We spend our time writing guidelines, monitoring policies, or investigating interview practice but it has been hard to interest anyone in talking about how we might facilitate others or create opportunities for disabled employees. Not long ago, I sat in a meeting whilst the head of the Equal Opportunities Unit, who knows of my disability, presented all his information on the overhead projector with microscopic tables to illustrate the difficulties faced by students from ethnic minority groups with few academic qualifications. The meeting was entirely inaccessible to me. When my own rights are so blatantly ignored, it is hard to empathise with other marginalised people, and this makes me feel selfish, paltry and ill-suited to my role.

Equal opportunity policies in organisations like the one in which I work are overwhelmingly about gender and race, with disability issues being 'tagged on' almost as an afterthought. In my own experience the notion that such policies exist has raised expectations with little result. Equality must be part of the very fabric of the organisations in which we work. This has considerable resource implications and it will mean radical changes to the social, physical and political structures of work.

Until this happens, it is important to remove the empty and dishonest rhetoric even if it means returning to the bluntness and ruthlessness of the bad old days. I found it a whole lot easier when I was told I could expect nothing and sometimes found there was something after all.

Ann Macfarlane

Watershed

We were quiet, hiding our fear
Knowing in our nine-year-old hearts
That we were about to witness something
Frightening and evil.
One cried quietly,
And we clutched inadequate towels around our thin bodies
As Mary, pretty and small, passive and unmoving
Became the focus of all our attention.

They lifted her effortlessly
Into the deep porcelain tub
And then, without warning
Pushed her passive pale body under the water
And held her there.
We felt the fear through our ill-clad bodies.

There was no shriek, no cry, no dramatic action.
The loud clock ticked on
A reminder that we had seen this before,
Had shivered, cried restlessly
And watched Mary come up again.
Now we were two weeks more knowing
And understood that we must not move,
Must not show what we felt.

Mary was dead.
Her body naked in the porcelain bathtub,

Tiny, frail, utterly lifeless.
Her long wavy hair over her face
Not pretty any more.
She was so fragile.
She needed to be hugged, needed to be cared for.
But her bathers had no compassion.
They stood motionless over her,
Eyes staring transfixed
Not seeing a human child, not seeing her.

Slowly their attention turned outwards to us,
Unacknowledged, unwanted onlookers.
One by one we were wheeled back to our beds
Alone with our fearful thoughts.
No one spoke of Mary again.
It was as if she had never been,
And yet she was our friend,
Part of our lives.

Nearly fifty years later, this scene comes and visits me.
Then, we knew we must stay silent.
Now I speak it for all the Marys
In institutions, in hospitals, in segregated schools
And for my nine-year-old self, who had no choice
But to sit and watch.

Merry Cross

Abuse

'Do you really expect us to believe that anyone could want to have sex with a smelly shitty child like you?' If a (defence) lawyer can speak this way to a disabled child in the witness box at their abuse trial, where can we turn to block out the din?

'This is probably part of some rare syndrome.' If a doctor can write this on the case notes of a disabled girl on whose body he has just noted anal and vaginal tearing and bruising, where can we turn to heal our wounds?

When Canadian statistics show over 50 per cent of both boys and girls reporting abuse in a residential school for deaf youngsters, and a 1991 English study uncovered that 98 per cent of a group of 148 adults with learning difficulties reported contact sexual abuse, where can we turn to shelter our eyes from the glare?

These quotes and statistics have come to my notice over the past three years as an increasing amount of my work has begun to focus on the area of disability and child abuse. It started with a 'chance' invitation to speak at probably one of the first conferences on disability and child abuse in this country. There I met Margaret Kennedy, the only worker in England whose sole job description was to work on the abuse of disabled (in this case deaf) young people.

We have worked together closely ever since, first on a disability working party of the British Association for the Study and Prevention of Child Abuse and Neglect, on the newly formed United Kingdom Coalition on Disability and Abuse, and more recently as part of a wider consortium developing a training package on the subject for the Department of Health. As two disabled women, we have had no difficulty understanding each other or complementing each other's work. All that I heard confirmed the impression I'd gained over years in the disability movement, that abuse is the rule, rather than the exception, in the experience of disabled people.

In a sense it is startlingly simple. We live in a world which depends for its smooth functioning on marginalising all those for whom its living, working and leisure space was not designed. But we are not just marginalised, we are oppressed, and the oppression and abuse have one central identical effect – to make the victims blame themselves and feel that they are bad.

It's a theme that I and my friends have explored repeatedly over the years, especially those of us who were born with our conditions. One disabled friend, ill in bed at boarding school, had to lie quietly as the matron forced a boy on top of her. A young girl was made to stand almost naked in front of two male strangers who took photos – on the orders of the hospital consultant. A deaf girl was beaten and forced to do all the housework for a large household, on the grounds that that was all she'd ever be good for. A tiny girl was just one of the disabled children on a ward abused physically and sexually by a night nurse. Perpetrators can often still depend on the silence that ensues from threats, from depending on their help, from the disbelief of others.

And it isn't easy to draw a line between oppression and abuse. Isn't it abusive to use disabled people in fiction as metaphors for evil (the wicked witches and evil pirates, for example)? And isn't it abusive to describe someone's blind eye as their *bad* eye? No wonder so many of us, abused or not, half kill ourselves trying to prove how *good* we are! Sometimes it seems that for those of us who have been abused, no amount of proof will ever be enough.

Perhaps it is the sheer depth of pain and horror around abuse that prevents the disability movement from reaching *first* deep into the heart of the institutions for disabled people, youngsters and adults alike. For there, at the centre of the oppression, lie also those most abused of our number. There are the ones who are chosen because they cannot speak of the horror. There are the ones who are chosen because they cannot run away, and there is nowhere to run. There are the ones who are chosen because their very lives depend on not fighting back. There are the ones who are chosen because there is no one for them to tell. There are the ones who are chosen because no one has even taught them the words. There are the ones who are chosen because society chooses to believe that, after all, they don't really have any sexuality, so it can't hurt them.

One has only to read what perpetrators say about how they select their victims to grasp rapidly that as a society we more or less set disabled youngsters up as perfect targets. Segregated; isolated; rejected; in the hands of a plethora of carers who are employed without vetting, their bodies handled as adults see fit; called by their equipment ('He's a catheter'), their conditions ('She's a CP'), or procedures necessary in their care ('She's a toileter') – in fact almost anything except their names; deprived of respect, we may as well dress them in clothes which announce 'COME AND GET ME'.

And now there is the battle to get the new Children Act amended, so that it can encompass the realities of working with our abused little ones, rather than just describing them pompously as having 'special needs' and then only paying lip service to those needs. For instance, the time allowed for assessment interviews is hopelessly inadequate for most disabled children (especially those who use non-verbal communication).

It hurts. Some of us cannot remember. Some of us wish we could forget. Some of us wouldn't dream of calling the doctor who regularly put his hand up our skirts without a word of permission or explanation, an abuser. Some of us wouldn't dream of calling the physiotherapist who strapped us into agonisingly painful equipment, despite our cries, an abuser. It was all for our own good.

That's what they all say.

My sisters, the pain lessens a little when we talk about it, cry about it, rage about it, with someone who understands. It lessens more when we act to prevent it, in whatever ways we can. One of the most important things we can do is make relationships with our young ones and help them know their bodies, their worth, their beauty, their absolute right to respectful treatment at all times – and to know that *we* at least will believe them. Another, of course, is to act together to challenge and dismantle the oppression, as many of us do already.

Does the pain ever go away? I don't know. Reach in to those who cannot reach out, and perhaps we will find the answer together.

Jenny Morris

The Fall

There have been two falls in my life.

The first was the fall from grace when I was two or three years old. I don't know exactly when it happened, I can't even remember it happening. But I have grown up with the feeling of it, deeply rooted inside me. I became a problem, disapproved of, no longer a beautiful baby but a troublesome toddler. A bewildered, grieving, bottomless cavern of need.

I'm not sure precisely what caused this fall. My brother was born when I was almost two and that must have been part of it. Partly, though, it was my parents' reaction to the inevitable passing of the specialness that all babies have. Having experienced this now as a mother myself, I know how difficult it is for unconditional love, so easy to give to a baby, to survive. It was a long time before I recognised that my mother must have given such love to me when I was a baby. For many years I could not believe that I had ever been loved. My memories are of disapproval, anger, cold isolation. I have no recollection of either of my parents touching me with affection.

This paralysed me as I grew into adulthood. I had no foundation of self-esteem, little sense of self-worth, and I lurched through a series of unsatisfactory relationships as I sought to plug the gaping hole of emotional need which was the legacy of my childhood.

Somehow I thought the second fall would wipe out the first – that when I fell off that wall and literally paralysed half my body my mother would finally look after me, nurture me without question, heal my emotional hurt.

The power of this reaction – *now* my mother will have to look after me – was such a shock to my thirty-three year old mature (I thought) self that I spent several months after the accident examining whether I had somehow deliberately created the situation. The fear that I had filled me with terror.

In any case, my mother didn't react by wanting to look after me. She stood by my bed and said very little. There was no greater feeling between us, no mitigation of the nothingness which was by then at the heart of our relationship. Her own emotional paralysis was all too clear. Whenever I expressed a need for help – a request that she talk to the consultant at the hospital, or an attempt to share with her some of my feelings as I lay there with my life apparently in ruins – I drew a complete blank. She had no resources with which to respond.

I had thought that as a mother she would at least connect with the circumstances of my fall. For me, becoming a mother had opened up a capacity for caring, for being vulnerable to a concern for others, particularly children. When I saw that child stuck on the ledge by a railway line I felt as if my own child was in danger. My instinctive reaction was that of a mother. But my own mother did not respond to this – I felt no echo of maternal concern in her, and there was no identification with what had happened to me as I lay in that hospital bed, grief-stricken at the separation from my daughter.

For a long time I went on hoping. A year after the accident it became finally clear that she didn't have anything to give me. We had gone out to the local park, my mother, Rosa – then two – and me. I was on a three-wheel scooter, with Rosa on my knee, when suddenly the scooter overbalanced on the steep gradient and we were in a heap on the grass. My mother froze. She just stood there. She couldn't – with either body or words – even express concern. It was a passer-by who leapt into the situation saying, 'How awful for you, let me help.' I had felt such panic at this sudden reminder of my physical vulnerability, but there was no space for me to express it. After comforting Rosa I had to make it all right for my mother, who had just not known what to do.

I never stopped wanting her to be my mother in the period between my accident and her death four years later. My physical paralysis had reawakened my emotional need for her but in fact it was I who had to struggle to meet *her* needs. It was a familiar situation. When I had been at boarding school, I used to receive letters from her full of misery, to which I wrote supportive replies, hoping that the holidays would bring us closer together. But a thirteen year old has little to offer a woman in her late thirties struggling with the after-effects of an unnecessary hysterectomy and a deep feeling of unfulfilment at the centre of her life. So the closeness I so desperately wanted never happened.

During the year she was dying of cancer, I did the practical things. I helped her to find out about the drugs she was prescribed, helped her to get the support she needed, told her GP that she wanted to die at home. Yet I didn't take care of her and that was only partly because of my physical paralysis. My father looked after her, with the same high standards that he applied to everything.

During that year she never expressed her love for me or gave me any indication that I was important to her. I will always remember sitting in her kitchen with her while she filled out a form for the Bristol Self Help Cancer Centre. The form asked about any emotional traumas she might have experienced during the previous five years. I sat there, feeling importantly guilty, waiting for her to say, 'Well, of course there was your accident.' After all, your only daughter breaks her back when her own child is thirteen months old – how much more traumatic can you get? *Now* she would acknowledge my significance to her. But no. Instead she spoke of my younger brother's unsettled life and her worries about him. Inside I was saying, 'What about me?'

On the afternoon before she died, I sat beside the single bed my father had set up for her in a small ground-floor room overlooking the garden. An old desk which used to belong to my grandfather was next to the bed and I couldn't get my wheelchair very near to her. The footplates stuck out, and the nearer I tried to move, the more I worried about scraping the desk and my father's disapproval. 'I'll miss you,' I said, 'I can't get close enough to kiss you.' 'Any excuse,' she replied with a vague, weak smile. Was it? I had always thought that the reluctance to have physical contact had come from her.

At the funeral I cried, the only one in my family who did. But not for her – at least not for what her absence would mean to me. The loss I experienced had been there for years. And I suppose that's what I cried for at her funeral.

But as the years have passed and I have made more sense of my life, I realise that the consequences of those two falls – the emotional impairment and the physical paralysis – are part of an experience which I value. In this, the tenth year since my accident, I celebrate so many things. There is movement in my life – the development of ideas about impairment and disability, the progress which myself and other disabled people are making in the growth of our self-esteem, our self-confidence, our conviction of the importance of disability as a human and civil rights issue. There are feelings in my life – the love I have for my daughter, the closeness I experience with the people who are important to me, the passion I have for the work I do. And I celebrate what I feel about myself.

My first fall left me feeling worthless and unattractive. It fundamentally undermined my sense of self-worth. The second catapulted me into a social group – 'the disabled' – whose perceived inadequacies deny us our worth as human beings. In struggling against the consequences of the second fall, I have laid the ghosts of the first.

My physical impairment is not something I would choose. I would rather be able to walk than have to use a wheelchair. I would rather the spasm in my legs didn't wake me up at six o'clock in the morning. I would rather I didn't have to worry about incontinence when I share a bed with someone. I would rather I didn't have the burning sensation in my legs which is there every waking moment of my day – and night. Yet I love how I am and the life I lead. I like what I see when I look in the mirror. I value so much the contact I have with other disabled people – and with non-disabled allies – in our struggle against prejudice and discrimination. But most of all, I celebrate that I am not the mother to my daughter that my mother was to me. Whatever mistakes I make, I will not repeat that nothingness between us.

There is no emotional paralysis at the centre of my relationship with my daughter. Rosa has a deep anger against me for our separation when she was thirteen months old and it took a long time to regain the specialness of our relationship which had characterised for me the first year of her life. But my love for her is unconditional; it recognises that she is the most important thing in my life but it also celebrates her separation from me. An eleven year old, going on fifteen, she is straining to be independent, insisting that she knows best, wanting to do things differently from her mother. None of this changes my love for her.

Ten years ago I had little understanding of all this. My mother's reaction to my accident forced me to realise that the needy two year old inside me had to love and nurture herself. In looking after myself in the aftermath of physical paralysis, I am now able to look after my daughter in a way which, I hope, will give her a sense of her own worth as a human being, a self-esteem which I have taken so long to gain for myself but which I now celebrate in my identity as a disabled woman.

Emily Oxford

Prue Shows Her Knickers

Prue was just a teenager. She was skinny and lean but two budding breasts made faint bumps under her clothes. Boys teased her and Andy kept asking for a flash.

The once-soft face of childhood was harder now, her jaw jutted forward a little, a physical sign of her stubbornness. Circumstance had made her wilful, wary and nervous of the world she lived in, but somewhere the indomitable spirit of her optimism still burned.

She was not normal. She was a cripple, she was handicapped, she was a Special pre-pubescent.

Her legs were unique maps of her illness, stiff and unbending, her knees decorated with tiny craters and variously swelling bumps. She didn't walk on them much and used a wheelchair at times she called simply 'agony' days. Her neck, though rarely painful, bent to one side and stayed there. These were her bodily impairments which attracted the labels of doctors, and consequently categorised her neatly for the rest of the world.

The labels attached to her had done their work; her psyche suffered its own impairments as a result, and as she approached adolescence, she found herself nervous about a world which had once seemed a dazzling dance of magic.

She never thought much about her situation, she just accepted that she was these things other people placed on her, and if it kept the peace with her anxious, fretting mother, then she played by the rules that meant she saw lots of white-coats, went to a Special school in a Special bus and didn't expect to do a whole array of things in the hostile, anti-cripple world.

But even these rules had begun to change of late.

Now she was expected to play the Independence game – a game with a particular definition. Lectures on 'Personal Independence' featured in her life these days with growing regularity. She had to go to 'Buttons and Bows' classes, where groups of bored teenagers were grilled about how to tie shoe laces; tackle buckles, poppers, buttons, zips; pull this on, pull that off; and sundry other activities. With her twig-like fingers curving at bulbous joints that neither bent very far nor had the strength to stay straight, most of these tasks were to Prue a punishment in ritualised boredom. She knew her own limits, just as she knew what challenges were worth taking on. These activities were pointless and demoralising as she failed at every attempt. The 'teachers' – in fact blue-coats serving under the Head's baleful glare – would tut at her and admonish her to try harder.

The enforced ideas about Independence were suffocating shadows closing in on her life. She had to be taught to do everything in her life herself, absolutely, in readiness for adulthood when there would be no kind mum to wait on you, no teachers and Care ladies, oh no. It seemed to Prue it was the sort of Independence you might only need if you were the only person left alive on some fantastic, civilised desert island; and it was the sort of Independence which she knew she could never actually achieve.

What being Independent meant, of course, was being able to present to their real world an approximation of Normality. You wouldn't ever have to bother a nice Normal person with your nasty difficulties, you'd never have to ask for anything. It didn't matter how many hopeless hours of pain and toil were involved.

But who was she to argue? She was just a cripple kid, told every day that she didn't know what was best for herself, in her Special situation . . .

If you didn't play the game of Independence by their rules, they made fearful threats about putting you in a Home when you reached sixteen. It was up to you, they would shrug, as if they had no say in the decision. If you tried your hardest and were Independent, then you didn't have to worry. You would be allowed into their world.

But spring hung in the air, a fresh breeze of hope tickling clouds across the sky. In the kitchen, the chunky radio burbled low-volume pop music as Audrey sat at the table filing her nails, and Prue's baby brother Rory methodically devoured his bread soldiers.

'Not feeling too bad about school today, are we?' Audrey asked, lifting dark eyes to her daughter. 'It being the last day and that.'

'No mum, I just want it to be over with.' Prue glared at her toast, charcoaled at one edge where her mum had forgotten to take it out from under the grill in time.

With her husband some time gone, Audrey was a typical prematurely faded beauty. She moved in slow motion, swimming in a pool of deep warm memory. Her absent-mindedness now revealed itself as dreamy self-preoccupation. She never quite heard conversations directed at her first time around. Her eyes were focused on the middle distance, catching on Pete's photos which she had plastered on the walls of their increasingly shabby house.

She pulled back a long strand of unbrushed hair, a seaweed swirl of deep colour no longer piled high on her head.

'I know you're worried about tomorrow, but it won't be too bad. You're a big girl now, used to all these things.'

Oh yeah sure, Prue thought, shuddering at the idea of what was to come.

Audrey pushed herself up wearily, hands flat on the table.

'I dare say they won't keep you long, Prue, I promise –.'

'Don't promise, don't promise!' Prue snapped, giving up on the leathery rag of toast. 'You always do that, you always promise and you don't mean it, you don't know what you're saying!'

Audrey's eyes dropped away, scanning the pebble tablecloth. She stood very still, rooted with sudden hurt.

'I was about to promise to visit you once a week, Prue. I can't promise you anything else, can I? I don't know what's going to happen to any of us . . .'

She trailed away, feet slopping across the lino.

Prue knew what she meant. Since her dad had died they had had little control over their lives. Her hard heart felt the soft bruise of regret at her quick stern words to her mother, but she couldn't apologise. She was always sniping away at mum, always saying the wrong things.

Prue had to draw on every ounce of her hard-won reserve of strength today because two traumas were facing her at school. The white-coat prodders had decided to send her away to a new place for 'better treatment', so this was her last day for God knows how long. She would be going to another hospital. They all kept insisting that it wasn't a hospital – even her mother – but a special residential centre for children and young adults with arthritis; just what she needed. But Prue was not calmed by their explanations. She had grown weary and resigned towards their soothing platitudes and downright lies. With a churning in her stomach, she braced herself for the worst.

But although this imminent event lay in her mind like a heavy, dulling ache, there was a more pressing engagement awaiting her at school.

She had been half dared, half coaxed into promising Andy Easter a look down her knickers – as long as she was allowed a look down his. She and Sally had giggled over the prospect all week, and in high bravado she had announced the forthcoming exploit for days. Now the whole class knew about it, and boys and girls alike laughed and chattered expectantly as she entered the classroom.

Sally was excited and anxious, a great bubbling jitter of worry.

'What if you're caught? What if they tell your mum?'

'Mum won't care, she knows I'm not stupid. I'd say it was just a silly game. Anyway, we won't get caught – he's only getting a few seconds look! That's the dare!'

Sammy Smith, one of their gang, a small compact tomboy of a girl with twisting wiry hair, pulled a face.

'You'll have to watch him, 'e's a bugger! Don't let him touch nothin'! If 'e does I'll whack him for yer!'

Sammy was tough, renowned for hurtling down the corridors on her three-wheeled walking frame, scattering unwary younger pupils as she went.

'Oh blimey, no touching, course not!' Prue laughed, hiding the lurch in her stomach which reminded her suddenly not only of the present embarrassing scrape she was in, but also of her appointment with new white-coats tomorrow. She could hardly believe that she was leaving all her friends, Miss Tobin, and her mum and brother, for who knew how long. And thoughts of her mum brought back the painful scene at breakfast.

Andy was grinning at her across the classroom, tapping his flies with the palm of his hand, a swanking display for his sniggering mates. She pulled a disgusted face at him before turning back to the gang. At least there was a morning full of lessons before she had to Do It.

No one was allowed to watch, they both insisted on that, meeting inside the stationery cupboard, at the edge of the assembly hall. Their friends waited outside, giggling and hushing each other, keeping a sharp watch for teachers or prowling Snotty Scott.

Prue had worked herself up into a perfect state of arrogant devilry, deciding this was the only way she could get through the ordeal. Anyhow, her mother had taught her not to be ashamed of anything to do with her private parts (although she didn't like Prue to display her bumpy lumpy legs), saying that they were hers and she should be proud to be a woman.

Now here she was, wearing her best pink knickers, facing Andy and staring him in the eye, allowing him no chance to renege on his part of the dare. He looked up at her, sheepish now the door was shut, his grin not so swanky.

'Well?' said Prue, keen to get it over with. Mum might have told her to be proud of her 'Miss Mary' but at this instant she felt silly and embarrassed.

'Who's going to go first, then?' he asked uncertainly, playing with the top of his trousers.

'We'll do it together. Let's count to three, then – then show ourselves – only for five seconds – we'll count together.'

Her stomach was doing somersaults. A tiny voice somewhere asked her why she was being so childish. It was too late to answer that.

Andy had his hands ready at his zip. Prue hooked her stiff fingers with some difficulty into her knickers. Looking down at him, a pang of pity hit her. What a sorrowful sight he was. He was terrified! But being a boy he couldn't let on, could he? She felt strong and in charge. Why was she afraid? She'd seen a willy, on Rory and in books. His couldn't be any more peculiar or strange. She decided to display herself with a flourish.

'Right then ... get ready, let's count together ... one ... two ... three!'

A quick extra second of struggle with unwieldy clothes and there they stood.

'One chim-pan-zee, TWO chim-pan-zee ...' Prue stared hard at the grey-pink length of flesh that lay limp and wrinkled in Andy's hand. She wanted to laugh but managed a less insulting smile instead, noticing that Andy was avidly looking down as she held her dress under her chin. She stepped back slightly, her legs moving apart. His willy looked like a sagging sausage that was going off she decided, and those straggles of hair around it, yuck!

'... FIVE chim-pan-zee!' they chorused together before hastily covering themselves. Outside the others were growing restless. Andy still looked nervous.

'Er ... it's not very big, is it? I mean, my brother has got a really huge one.'

Prue wanted to laugh out loud. She was going away from all this tomorrow, and she knew how much she would miss it. She would even miss Andy.

'Well, I don't really know. It looked just the same as the others I've seen,' Prue remarked airily, amazed at how timid he had become in displaying his prized part to her. 'How did I do?'

She didn't actually care much what he thought but was interested in what he might say.

He looked up at her, taller as she was, and smiled shyly.

'You're great, Prue. I really like you. You're pretty.'

Prue was flabbergasted by this response, expecting something rude and smart. But she was in control and she knew it. She also knew now that the great, bragging, flashy bugger Andy Easter had never seen a woman's private part before. She glowed and smiled.

'You're all right too, mate.' There was a little devil suddenly inside her. Tomorrow this would all be gone ... for a long time, she just knew it.

'Give us a kiss, then.' The words came out of her mouth, a dancing request half-filled with laughter, half with blank nerve. She bent down to him, put her hand on his shoulder, and pressed her lips against his.

She didn't want him to forget her in a hurry while she was away.

Janice Pink

Do Unto Others

I was waiting at the checkout and leaning on my crutch
When a voice behind me loudly said, 'Come, come, this is
   too much!

'Hey, Miss,' she called. 'Young lady! I say! Now listen,
   dear,
You'd better get a move on, we've got a cripple here!'

The cashier's tapping fingers stopped, she looked around
   to see
Who this pathetic creature was – I realised it was *me* ...

'Now let me help unpack your load – the least that I can do –
Because, but for the grace of God, I could be just like you!

'Does anybody help you? Or do you live alone?
Oh, do you buy this in a tin? I always bake my own.

'You haven't got a husband? Well, build a social life –
Perhaps you'll meet a crippled man who wants a crippled wife!'

I found this quite offensive, and told her so, at length,
She said, 'My dear, I understand – you've lost your health
   and strength.

'I know you're being very brave, but that *was* rather rude –
Next time someone helps you, try to show some gratitude.

'Of course you think life isn't fair, but when you're feeling
   blue –
Big smile! And then remember, there's someone worse
   than you!'

Aspen

What Did You Soy?

Do you get your nongue in tots? Is your life full of herbal goofs? Do you 'Tune off the televasion', or say 'Hello Knickers' to Nicky? Do you try to buy 'fruit guns' or 'jeans with electrocuted waists'? Do you eat 'a bowl of sellotape' for breakfast and ask your partner to 'Sass the mugar'? I do. It's enough to make me suck.

It affects my smelling – I mean 'spelling'. 'Anybordy' is my favourite, but 'pay-nut' and 'hoing gome' come close. I can't get my gear into brain.

I recently warned a friend she was 'Making a rod for her own bath'. I told another to 'Avoid it like a bargepole'. 'You want your face and eat it,' I admonished. It just goes to show how long you can be.

Romance is not spared . . . watching a sunset with my partner, I murmur 'You don't get evenings like *this* on a plate'. 'I lug you' is so passionate, don't you think?

That suns it up wall. Mostly I loff but sometimes I get fed enough.

ps If you knees an explanation write to me personably. If you want a replay, send a stomped addressed envelope.

Liz Crow

Day in the Life of Liz

Dear Ju,

Well, this is a sure fire way of making me do something constructive with my time. I'm stranded somewhere between the first and third floors of the polytechnic. Yes, you've guessed it: after so many months of threatening to strike, the lift has finally caught up with me. It's okay at the moment – being confined in a four feet by four feet metal coffin hasn't got to me so far – and hopefully this will at last spur them on to fork out on repairs. A member of the library staff got stuck last term (for over three hours). The powers-that-be got a bit touchy about that; the idea of a *disabled* student being stuck should really put the wind up 'em! The library staff are being very sweet. They keep talking to me and clearly have visions of panic setting in. Meanwhile, PTL for personal computers ...

That was the library staff again: 'Are you still all right? Would you like us to stay and talk to you?' 'No, no, I'm fine.' (It's knackering bellowing up and bellowing down a lift shaft.) 'I have my computer, so I'm okay.' 'You have your computer in there? – She has her computer in there!' relayed to the rest of the staff.

My whole life seems to revolve around access (lack of) at the moment. I tried to go to the Museum of the Moving Image last week – *their* lift is out of order, but anyway, it seems their 'accessible route' means going through the entire exhibition backwards in order to reach the starting point, so I think I'll boycott that one. I found a council health club with swimming, massage and jacuzzi, and went to check out the facilities yesterday, but *they* couldn't work out how to operate the stairlift, so I went back home. It all reminds me of my first day at the poly when the very first thing I managed to do was get firmly wedged between the 'accessible' loo and the 'accessible' loo door and had to press the panic button to be released.

Twenty minutes later and they've rung for the outside lift engineers. I must remember to request the installation of a wall-table and a potty.

I'm bad, having taken on too much, but too tempting not to, so hope no regrets two weeks from now! There's the biggest UK disability rally yet – three major cities and upwards of fifteen thousand people expected (not bad going considering lack of accessible transport, money, personal assistance, and so on). Today I volunteered to get together the banners and placards for the London contingent, so now I have to organise a group, materials and design, and make it all happen. Two-hundred-plus placards, all for around fifty quid. Regrets? Hah!

The whole demo thing is beginning get under way at last in this country, though we need to make the whole thing more cohesive/unified/impact-ing. Our techniques are relatively unsophisticated compared to other civil rights groups because our mass protest is still all so new. But last week there was another bus blockade of Oxford Street ('At Last Disabled People Are Catching Buses' read the banner) which resulted in 'seventeen people being arrested, eleven in wheelchairs', i.e. publicity at last.

The publicity was really useful to us: when 'our' lawyers requested the cases be moved to an accessible court this was refused, so there were (local) TV pictures of people being carried into the court. The justice system looked proper silly and the media comments were well favourable to us.

I have to decide whether to steward on this rally, or whether to go and demonstrate; in which case it could be law abidance versus arrest. Not sure how I feel about getting arrested. But what with this and the poll tax, I'm sure to find out some day soon.

The lift engineers haven't turned up, so they're now calling the fire brigade!

On the subject of arrests, I heard a bulletin from Parliament the other week. Apparently the Home Office is now implementing plans for wheelchair-accessible facilities in Britain's jails. (Out of the local authority prison, into the Home Office one.) Nice to know they have their priorities straight. Personally, I think this is directly related to the first big national disability demo two years ago which brought half of South London to a halt. Rumour has it that it really put the shits up them to see disabled people out there (even shouting and waving placards!). The response is certainly logical and demonstrates an unassailable commitment to equal opportunities.

Oh shit, I can hear sirens!!
Hiss of brakes and grind to a halt.
Clunk, clunk.
(Tell you what, sod the lecture after this. I'm heading straight for the bar. As soon as I've been to the loo.)

Ever-ripe for a bit of masochism, I've just been to the bi-annual NAIDEX (national aids for 'The Disabled' Exhibition). As ever, it was all able-bodied – able-bodied designed, able-bodied run; scores of able-bodied, white, middle-class, suited men. And full of so many ugly images. There are able-bodied salesmen having a laugh, racing up and down on wheelchairs and on scooters – till it suits them better to walk, when up they leap. Body-beautiful females ('Miss Everest and Jennings'), swimsuit-clad, model bath hoists to hoards of long-tongued, lusting salesmen. And the aids and equipment are priced so high they're out of the range of all but the rich and famous. I need eighteen grand – not 'would like' but 'need'. Now I wonder, which shall I apply to: Telethon or the DSS Social Fund?

... Clunk ...

The manufacturers, of course, have us over a barrel. As long as the government refuses to resource essential needs, how can we not spend our last pennies on their goods? My only comfort was the exhibition's poor security. So easy 'twould be to trial a demo-wheelchair in the direction of the nearest exit sign and never return. I have no moral hesitation, knowing the way they line their pockets from our predicament. My only fear would be getting caught. But then, imagine the headlines: 'Cripple Caught Stealing Mobility'. (Can you steal a right?) And prosecuting a poor defenceless cripple would be *so* bad for business.

Lowering of chains? (Disturbing the peace and quiet and the clickety click click of my letter writing.)
Doors opened. Man lowering? (God, this is embarrassing!)
Silence.
Does this sort of thing happen to other people?

Money (or the lack of it) seems to be dominating my life at the moment. I'm just putting together my final final appeal for attendance allowance. If you can prove that you need full-time 'attendance and supervision' you might (might) win enough cash to pay for approximately six hours' assistance per week. I've been turned down (lies, damned lies from the DSS medical examiners) at two stages so far and have received a provisional 'no' at the final hurdle, despite my chances actually having looked good for a time. So much for counting chickens: I'd been counting pennies and pounds (over two-and-a-half years' back-pay). I'd visualised presents all round for my glee club, with a holiday in the sun for me to recuperate from the strain of it all. And the anticipation of relieving my financial straits felt fine. Pfffh!

So now I've got my last-ditch attempt to plead, beg, prostrate myself, etc. I've spent a demoralising month keeping a diary of every last thing I can't do (plus some more), written reams (well, nine pages) giving a blow-by-blow account of a day in the life of . . . (when all else fails, try wearing them down). I'm submitting letters from various Professionals as evidence, including a letter from the housing co-op's newly invented 'tenant support officer' (a mate of mine, bless 'im!). And Mum has just written a supremely brilliant and heart-rending account of her daughter's disintegration – when she read it to me over the phone I near-wept to hear of this poor woman's plight (mine, I mean, tho' perhaps it should be hers too). So, if that doesn't do the trick, I give up. All this angst for twenty-four quid a week.

Many more clunks, forcing of doors, shoutings up and shoutings down, and . . .

. . . And four burly and rather good-looking firemen – water-proof trousers, leather gloves, shiny yellow helmets and all – got me out. 'See you again,' one of them said (tho' I don't think *that*'s what he meant). I hope not!

But it didn't end there. Because I spent the rest of the evening being hauled from floor to floor by human lifts (never quite reaching the floor with the bar on it), and somewhere between the third floor and my car I lost my house keys, but didn't realise till I got home, by which time the college switchboard had closed down, and the housing co-op's spare keys could not be found but my neighbour went and collected my other spare keys from my home help, whilst my other neighbour plied me with wine, but when I put them in my brand-new 'accessible' lock, I found the lock had jammed and I had no way into my flat so, my other, other neighbour went to hunt out a screwdriver . . .

But, in the meantime, the lock clicked into place and I was *home*!

I am *home*!! (Why did Mum laugh?)

So after that fairly standard day in the life of Liz, I shall leave you. See you again ever so soon.

Lots of love,

Liz

Jaihn Makayute

Freedom Fighter

And the women whose fight
is with conviction against the disablers;
they look at me, they hear my desire,
and they say '*Scab*'.
And they say '*dreamer*' like it was a dirty word
and they say '*how dare she say such a thing*
how dare she say she wants to walk
again how dare she say she'd prefer
to run free, to feel her vagina again,
how dare she voice that
after all we've done to make
disability a state in which to be proud?'
And I say '*I dare to say*
such things
because they are my truth
and because I'm not scared now
of being burnt for voicing my truth,
I'm not afraid of being tortured
or ostracised by anyone
just for speaking
my truth.
My silenced-by-fear days are done.'

I say that
and I love myself
in this moment
without condition.

And I know how dreams come true.

And for this life
I am
truly
grateful.

And for freedom
my fight too
is with conviction.

Maria Jastrzębska

Warrior Woman

Lying propped up
on a large cushion
in my woolly pink
dressing gown
is probably not
how you imagined her.

To be honest
I didn't either.
I rather fancied myself
dancing over hilltops
swirling swords in the air
all yells and flying kicks
or even leading
a mass protest rally
at least strutting my stuff
in trendy denim or leather
anything but like this.

Nevertheless
here I am
a warrior woman
in my pink dressing gown
dozing
or staring into space
watching the trees
through my window.

Imperceptibly
at first
ever so slowly
I am fighting back.

With every act of kindness
towards myself
every refusal
to blame
or despise myself
I strike back
against the men
in grey suits
who don't think
I'm cost effective
the ones in white coats
who don't even believe
I exist
all those too busy
or in too much of a hurry
to notice who I am.

From behind
my drooping eyelids
I am watching
with the stillness
of a lizard or snake.

I have learnt
the languor
and stealth
of a tiger
lying in wait
ready to pounce.

So next time
you come across

a woman like me
tired looking
in a pink dressing gown
just because
I'm lying low
don't imagine
I take anything
lying down.
Watch out
I have never been
as slow
or as deadly before.

Elsa Beckett

Taking Liberties

Above and around her the trees spread their lucent green, pure emerald fire caught from the sun. With dark trunks or silver-stemmed, they rose, carrying light toward the light. Underfoot the deep leafmould made walking slow as she climbed the slope, but she shunned the thin little path. Too many paths had already been shown her. She slipped and scrambled in this dappled light, working her way around exuberant bursts of undergrowth that tried to fill in the clearings, aiming towards the top of this little hill. As she reached it, however, her sickness took her, the colours and taste of it flooded and enfolded her in its inexorable embrace, pulling her tight into darkness.

When she came out of the black and sparkling depths of it, there were still the lambent leaves and cool air, glimpses of blue, and scents of earth and fungi and sweetness of the country, but over that and nearer the very human smell of Benar half-kneeling behind her, supporting her, hard shoulder in her back, breath on her neck, proffering a bottle of water. At first, when she had come up from the vortex, Benar would be standing apart from her, leaning against a tree, observing her dispassionately. And then, perhaps gaining courage or overcoming repugnance, she would help her to rise. But soon Dowlas would return to herself to find Benar already beside her, wiping her mouth and hands, brushing the leaves and twigs from her hair, all wordlessly and with the same lack of expression on her square, swart face.

When the sickness had first developed in Dowlas, several strategies had been employed to keep it as secret as possible. Her childhood was spent largely with distant relatives and, later, in the care of discreet governesses and teachers. In early youth she returned to her home at irregular intervals and for short periods, which she passed in an unfrequented wing of the house, rarely to be seen by servants. On attaining womanhood she was sent abroad to places where she and her family were unknown, though even then a false name was regarded as a wise precaution. This involuntary exile might have continued had not her uncle died and the control of power in the family shifted. Her cousin Aulis was not disposed to regard the sickness as such a source of family shame and had her brought home and installed in a comfortable little lodge on the estate – some distance from the house, it is true, but nevertheless near enough to allow of some intercourse with the family should she and they wish it. They did not.

Her servants were carefully chosen by her aunt and given meticulous instructions as to how she might live. She was neither to ride nor to swim. Moderate exercise was prescribed, but always under supervision. She should rest often. Her diet should be light, likewise her clothing. News of an exciting nature was to be kept from her, and her reading matter approved first by the aunt or the village priest. Aulis expressed some impatience with the latter stricture and would crate up books from the library at random and have them carried down to the lodge, or would from time to time order his bookseller to send a selection of current works. It may be that he felt some guilt at succeeding in position and wealth where his cousin was barred.

'What a cosy prison,' said Dowlas, shocking her housekeeper as she stepped over the threshold into the white-painted, deep-windowed little dwelling. 'No arrest and no trial, straight to the point. The new judiciary deserves more renown.'

She was, however, too indolent or indifferent to challenge her jailors. From what little she had known of her family she was not inclined to prolong the acquaintance. Her days passed in the way she was accustomed, with study, painting, walking, and correspondence with her old teachers.

Her new home, refurbished and decorated (albeit not to her own taste), was comfortable and she quickly resigned herself to her surroundings and isolation. Visits from friends she could not look forward to, except in very rare circumstances as when a scholar or writer might be in the locality.

The single diversion of the day was her walk, into the woods or along the river that led to the lake, up the wooded hill to the ruined little temple, or down across the meadow. Nature always brings something different and her delight in this was unaltering.

Benar, ex-kennelmaid, was assigned to accompany or rather follow her on these walks. It was among her duties to observe her charge, and, should an attack or aggravation of her illness occur, to render what little assistance was possible, to ensure she did not harm herself while in the throes of it and to summon help if this proved necessary. So each day the two set out, the first tall though not well-built, dressed with care but bare-headed, her long, light brown hair loosely bound, striding ahead confidently, ignoring, or perhaps hoping to outstrip the second woman, who was stocky, black-haired and rough-clad. Up the sunlit hill, into ferny woods or skirting the high-grassed fields, they went, pursuer and pursued, so it seemed. Dowlas chose the time for her perambulations when housekeeper and maid were engaged at the rear of the house, so no one witnessed this flight, or chase, or leading-and-following, which characters it assumed by turns.

She did not look behind to see if Benar followed, but took her own way heedlessly until she was out of sight of house and garden, and might proceed at a more leisurely pace, pausing to watch small creatures or to enjoy the aspect before her, or perhaps to pick a feral rose bright as a spatter of blood.

In time, and because of the apparent care shown her by Benar, she slowed her pace, and while they did not walk side by side, the appearance of it was somewhat companionable. They spoke rarely, to draw attention to deer or tree-rats, some striking plant, the red-skinned mushrooms. Once, when Dowlas had endured two seizures in one afternoon, she was distressed and despairing enough to drag herself, sweating and dirty, away from Benar, and say, 'Better to be done for. Not unwelcome to die in a place like this. I could hang from that tree there.'

Benar said sourly, 'And I should be out of a job.'

'Oh, you could get another position,' said Dowlas, surprised. 'My cousin would see to that.'

Benar glanced at her. 'You say that, who never had to find work.'

On another occasion, when Benar had to support her walking home, irked by her dependence Dowlas remarked irritably on the awkwardness of it, the difference in their heights being so great, and asked, 'Are *all* your people of your size?' She was discomfited by the reply: 'All but one, it seems. In the village is a man of your age and stature and with your face. Whether that makes him of my people or your people, who. decides?'

'I should like to see him,' said Dowlas, ruffled.

'You may look in the mirror to see him,' said the other curtly. 'He is not a curiosity for staring at.'

As they separated at the garden wall Benar added, 'Take my word, he is handsome. Had he not already chosen elsewhere, I would make a set at him myself.' But her tone was sarcastic and the look she directed at Dowlas disconcertingly sardonic.

Their familiarity with one another was of this limited kind, a rough exchange. Dowlas came to recognise two Benars, the dour person who followed or stood apart regarding her in a sometimes detached, sometimes brooding, way, and then the tender succourer who held and stroked her; who, after she had suffered a severe attack, fed her bitter chewed flowers, muttering the while some incantation or spell in her own language. These communions and ministerings, though unexpected, were neither embarrassing nor displeasing, imbued as they were with their own naturalness.

Her cousin was being courteous when he came to tell her of Benar's dismissal – after all, he could simply have replaced the woman without a word to Dowlas.

'The creature is insolent and disrespectful. You should have informed me. You were not obliged to tolerate her. We can't have people of her sort in our household.'

'How do you know how she is?' said Dowlas slowly.

There had been tales, spread by poachers, through villagers, through servants, of what transpired in the woods. It was not only her lack of deference; there were other irregularities, of conduct, between them; these had been seen.

'Of course, I know it was none of your doing – she obviously took advantage of your weakened state.'

'Did she say so?'

'She said nothing. She refused to give a yes or no. The effront-ery of her silence, the arrogance of it – were there nothing in the rumours, she certainly could not remain after this. When I insisted she speak, she sought to question me about some matter of your father and a village woman.' Reliving the confrontation, Aulis seemed no longer to care if anger and surprising disclosures would agitate Dowlas, she was amused to note. '*That*, she said, was the proper thing to be discussed and settled before all else.'

Dowlas was calm. 'She is surely right in that.'

Aulis stared. 'Your attitude seems to parallel hers. Do you defend her?'

'She has been of good service to me.'

'Were you whole, I would concede your right to be the judge of that,' said Aulis stiffly. 'As it is, your infirmity . . .' Abruptly, he changed direction. 'Do you understand, if formal accusations had been made it would be the gallows for both of you – yes, both, no privilege would protect you.'

Dowlas commented, 'Those who build and use the gallows are of course well-qualified to decide where and what love should be.'

'Love!' said Aulis. 'I hope I have seen enough of the world to recognise love in its various forms. When I questioned that barbarian there was nothing but overbearing pride on her ill-favoured face. How I hate these tribes. You see, it is true what is said; you can neither train nor trust them.'

The untrustworthy Benar was packing her few possessions when Dowlas sought her out in her room, only now seeing what mean quarters she had inhabited.

'I am sorry for this.'

'Not as much as I may be,' was the ungracious retort.

'Shall you go home?'

'Your cousin ensures I shall never get work in this region again. What is my choice but the city?'

'Then I choose that also.'

Benar tightened the rope on her pack. 'I can't support you,' she said harshly. 'It will be as much as I can do to shift for myself.'

'And I can't support you,' said Dowlas, equally angry. 'However, I can get us lodgings. I at least have some connections there. You, I would suppose, have none.'

With another change of name, she knew there would be no opposition to her leaving; while her people did all they could to keep her alive, her continuing existence dismayed them.

She softened her voice and said, 'I gather you would not be interrogated.'

'He asked questions that deserved no answer.'

Dowlas nodded. 'Nonetheless, he has made his own answers.'

'He wanted to believe. He was given what he wanted. Isn't that what servants are paid to do?' Benar grimaced her contempt.

They left the lodge singly and joined to travel together by night on the road through the village below. In the city Benar did portering, Dowlas copying and transcribing. In the grime and pallor of the city, far from their healthful homes, they were lovers for the first time, unless it was, after all, love that they had had before.

Appendix

Letters between the editor and Maria Jastrzębska,
Roz Rushworth and Ellie O'Sullivan

Lois and Maria

8 January 1993   Sussex

Dear Lois,

I was sorry to hear last summer from you of the loss in your
life. I hope you are finding a way through and regaining some
strength.

I am wondering if you've had a chance to do anything on the
anthology of writing by disabled women for The Women's Press
and if so, whether you're interested in using any of my work?
Is there a publication date for it? (It's eagerly awaited!)

Wishing you lots of health, optimism, hope and happiness for
1993,

With warm wishes,

Maria (JASTRZĘBSKA)

PS Please note my new address. (What a relief to have left the
Big City.)

14 January 1993   London

Dear Maria,

Thank you for your kind and supportive letter. It is only in the last few weeks that I have felt able to return to this project, but I am now attacking it with enthusiasm!

I met with my editor from The Women's Press for the first time a couple of weeks ago and we had a long and constructive talk about your writing which I had included in my sample to her. The poem I sent her to look at was 'Friends'. I thought you would like to hear her comments and hope that they don't seem too critical or negative. She said (and I agree with all this) that it was a broad, woman-centred and subtle poem with some lovely bits but that it left her with an uneasy feeling because of its passivity. This woman (you) is in an enforcedly passive position but why don't you express the anger you feel, why is it impossible to speak your mind to her – or even properly in her own head. Her question was – do you have any angrier poems? (!!) Do you?

I didn't show her 'Horns of My Dilemma' and this is a bit angrier but it's a quiet and subdued anger. I love the images of the fronds and bushy tails but I wondered if you would be willing to look at the second half of this poem again? I think it needs to be clearer what your disability is, what they see when they look at you, what you would like them to see. I love the last lines of this poem but the 'dilemma' isn't entirely clear.

I love your poem 'Suddenly I Am Very Ill' but in this anthology I am trying to focus not just on illness in a very personal way but on the political and social aspects of illness/ disability.

At the moment I am making a shortlist of work I am interested in, although I will not be making any final decisions until I have all the redrafts in. I would like to put these two poems on my shortlist and am keen to hear what you think about these comments and whether you'd like to look at them again.

I don't think that I will be able to use your 'Self Defence and ME' but have held on to it just in case. I hope that's okay. If you did have the time to rework it as you suggested in your June letter (so long ago!) so you were speaking directly to an audience who had bought a book of writing by disabled women, I'd be happy to look at it again.

Many thanks for your patience and I look forward to hearing from you soon,

Lois xx

28 January 1993   Sussex

Dear Lois,

Thank you for your letter and feedback on my work. Editors rarely have time for detailed criticism and having been on the other side too, I know how time consuming it is, so I really appreciate it, it's wonderful to get! I'm probably my own harshest critic so other people's comments are very useful.

Overall, I feel I'm getting a friendly kick up the bum from you to express more anger in my writing on the subject of disability/illness. It's funny but actually your letter feels timely in my life as a whole. Since I got your letter I've been going back to old poems and starting new ones and feeling inspired!

Having said that, I also want to put another view to you, partly to play devil's advocate but also because I believe it. Surely feminist/women's creative writing doesn't all have to be overtly militant, explicitly angry with strong heroines and neatly wrapped up triumphant endings. You seem to have a blueprint of how you'd like us to write but maybe we don't all fit into the mould!

I hope there will be some room in your book for sadness, loss, grief, frustration which are also part of our experience. One of the biggest issues, certainly for women with ME, is the isolation society imposes on us. Sharing our personal experience with one another is very much a political step towards breaking that isolation down. It's empowering to know someone else has gone through something similar and to have your experience named/ voiced/reflected.

As regards specific points on my poems: 'Horns of My Dilemma' – I agree with you about the second half entirely. Everyone loves the fronds (I'm partial to them myself!) but the second half is a bit of a mess. I will try to rework it and see what you think. I don't think I can be more specific about ME in this poem though, it needs to be general because it's on various levels. I've read it to lesbian audiences who immediately pick up on the invisibility issue. For me it's also about being Polish – so looking healthy and having a hidden disability, people assuming I'm heterosexual when I'm lesbian and that I'm English when I'm a Pole. This is too much to explain in one poem but I think I can do it another way.

'Friends' – Well, Lois, I like this poem! I don't feel I can tamper with it as it would spoil the flow. I don't think of the woman in it/me as being passive, rather as an observer. It *is* a quiet poem and a reflective one. This voice is part of an 'ME' voice as another woman with ME put it. There's something about being ill for a long time; you do a lot of watching the world go by and thinking, which the busy, 'healthy'/able-bodied folk don't have time for. Perhaps you are familiar with this.

The poem also begs two questions which I see as essential to the politics of illness, namely: who supports us women when we can't look after ourselves? and to what extent is ill health caused by the unhealthy stressful pace of life imposed on us? I know it doesn't set all this out in coherent essay form, but after all, it is only a poem! The only change I thought of making was to add a couple of lines at the very end and to make the rhythm more solid:

> this stillness
> after the curtains come down
> this is how tired woman
> without a moment
> to themselves
> define luxury.

Ironically, a few days after your letter came another woman told me she wished she had ME so she could stop!!

It's fine for you to hang on to the 'Self-Defence' piece. I've taken up some of the ideas in poem form and I'm sending you 'Warrior Woman' (!) and 'Poem to my Body' for you to have a look at. 'Horns' isn't ready yet. I don't know what sort of deadline you're working to but I've been rather slowed down by January flu.

Thanks again for your comments and care and for pushing me in a positive way. It's good to be in contact with you.

Warm wishes,

Maria

13 February 1993   London

Dear Maria,

There is such a lot I would like to say to you but as you acknowledge in your letter, the editor's job is a very time-consuming one and these days I'm trying to stick to business. Not always successfully!

Your letter was very interesting and the cat cartoon is on the noticeboard in my study. Your comments about what is political or strong in the writing by disabled women is very near to my own heart despite the impression I must have given in the comments about your poetry. I first started thinking about doing this anthology after I had read the American collection *With Wings*. I was doing a bit of research on it and talked to someone I know who is a lifelong campaigner on disability issues and has been disabled from birth. When I asked her what she thought of *With Wings*, which I had read from cover to cover, she replied, 'It's all about loss, I'm sick of loss, we ought to be moving on from that,' and I thought 'Oh dear, I'm still in loss and I don't know when I'm going to move on'. She is someone I really admire and I felt inadequate.

Like you I feel that this anthology has to include all the experiences of disabled women and some of that is about loss, pain and illness. My job is to balance it out so that there is also writing which is strong and positive and angry. Each piece has to be honest in its own terms. I suppose that when I made the comments about 'Friends', I was asking you whether you were comfortable about your role in this poem, were there things you wanted to say but chose not to? How do you feel when friends say they wish they had ME so they could stop? I know how I feel when people say to me that it must be great to be able to sit down all day!

I have reread 'Friends' and looked at 'Poem to my Body' and 'Warrior Woman'. I like them all but don't feel ready yet to make definite decisions so I'm just hanging on to it all. I would like to see any redrafts you make, I think the additional line in 'Friends' works well. Do you know the work of Aspen? She has also written about what the 'women pumping iron' scene makes her feel.

On a different note, I was talking the other day to the writer Gohar Kordi (*The Iranian Odyssey*) about her feelings about being blind and Iranian and quoted your line to her about not knowing whether you were ill in Polish or English and she really laughed and said, yes yes I know exactly what she means.

Anyway, Maria, I hope you are well and recovered from January flu. Perhaps one of these days we'll get to talk to each other although I know that you will understand if I don't respond quickly to anything else you might like to send me,

Best wishes,

Lois

1 May 1993   Sussex

Dear Lois,

Thank you for your open and lovely letter. It was good to hear your own thoughts on the loss v. anger debate. Actually I think you should use extracts from our correspondence in your book! They would surely express an important dilemma we have when writing about disability and I'm sure would strike chords for many women.

I feel my thinking about disability is still new. It's informed by my experience of other oppressions, being Polish, being a lesbian, etc., but it isn't the same. It's such a different kind of identity, having an illness. Despite prejudice I've encountered and internalised, deep down I *am* 'glad to be gay' as the song goes, proud to be a Pole, etc. But how can I be 'glad' to have ME?? I wouldn't wish it on anyone. (Well maybe a few politicians, bureaucrats, or doctors so that they wake up to some basic facts . . . !)

Also it's hard to separate out what's social and what's the pain of being ill sometimes. I do believe that in a different society it would be much, much easier to be ill – if you had the support you needed, but it wouldn't make the pain go away. And/but of course for me some good things have come out of having ME. One of the biggest is how it's turned my head around about disability. I think, pre-ME, disabled people were a 'Them' for me. I can't say I feel proud to have ME, but I do feel proud to be among other disabled people, to be part of 'us' does feel like a gift.

Well Lois, this is a bit of a jumble of thoughts, I hope they make sense. I must also apologise for taking so long to write back.

Last winter was a lousy time for me, but now it's spring and the daffs are out and I'm back in business.

I'd love to read some of your work and also I'm plotting in my mind how to get you and the book, when it's out, to Brighton for some kind of reading event. Just an idea . . .

Warmest wishes,

Maria

Lois and Roz

14 September 1992   Yorkshire

Dear Lois,

If I may call you that, I don't know if what I have enclosed is the type of thing you wanted but it was suggested at our writing workshop last Saturday that we each put our feelings on paper and sent them to you to do with as you will. The class was for women only, with disabilities. We found it a very useful exercise as we were able to express our feelings without embarrassment, speak more freely without the fellows there if you get my gist. I hope that doesn't sound sexist, it wasn't meant to as I enjoy the mixed groups very much.

I am fifty-nine years old and a grandmother. I have been a wheelchair user for three years, so I am a relative newcomer. I am also a member of a drama group called 'Mustn't Grumble'. We are putting on a review next month and I am involved in the writing and performing. It's great fun. I am also a member of the PHAB swimming club, so I'm pretty busy most of the time. (I wonder now how I found the time to work.) I am looking forward to your anthology when it's finished.

Good Luck,

Yours,

Roz Rushworth

10 October 1992   London

Dear Roz,

Thank you for sending me your writing. I enjoyed reading it
and thought that your simple, direct style worked very well in
creating a picture of yourself and your new life.

At the moment I am collecting work for a rather long shortlist
and would like to include your writing on that list, although
I'm afraid that it will probably be a long time before I am able
to make any final decisions.

I did think that the ending, where you are thinking about how
things could be improved for disabled people, read a bit like a
list and wondered if you could have a look at this again and
perhaps develop some of the ideas so that you maintain the style
of the rest of the piece. I'd be happy to read and give you my
comments on any changes.

I look forward to hearing from you,

Best wishes,

Lois Keith

23 October 1992   Yorkshire

Dear Lois,

Thank you so much for your kind letter, I am so pleased you
like my piece which I sent you. I can't tell you how thrilled I
will be if you do decide to put it in your book. I have kept a
rough copy of it. I read it through and decided to leave it alone,
except for the last paragraph which I have rewritten. I hope you
find this more acceptable. I have been told before that I am a
simple writer. I only write of what I know in a way which I
know. Some people enjoy it, others don't but that is the way
with people and of course their choice.

Some years ago when I was in America, I met up with a London publisher, she advised me to write of what I knew and not to feel bad about rejection. She told me that one day someone would like what I had written, so I keep on hoping that perhaps that will be true.

Thank you very much for your interest and good luck with the anthology.

Best Wishes,

Roz Rushworth

Lois and Ellie

20 December 1992   London

Dear Ellie,

How are you? I'm sorry that I haven't been in touch for such a long time. It isn't that I haven't been thinking about you but I have been rather overwhelmed by events at home this year. Over the last few months immediate domestic things have had to take priority and it's only recently that I have felt able to start working properly on the anthology again. I'm now making good progress but I know that this must have seemed like a long silence and I'm sorry.

I have been thinking a lot about your piece, 'The Visit', and I think it's very good indeed. I like the way you structured it within a contained space and time, I thought that worked very well. There are some great touches and the ending made me cry. I'm really glad you wrote it. However, I would like to make a suggestion and I hope that's okay. I don't know if you remember but when you were first thinking about this writing, we spoke about how you had always been very open with Charlotte about your cancer and the implications for both of you but found yourself unable to discuss your developing arthritis with her and how this silence surprised and upset you. I was wondering why you hadn't included this in your piece because it seemed an interesting and important idea.

I can imagine that this might be difficult but if you could look on this as a first draft and incorporate some of your thoughts about the different feelings you have about cancer and your developing arthritis, I do think it would work. Certainly it would highlight some ideas about disability and illness which none of other pieces I have received have done.

Let me know what you think. Perhaps we could meet and work on it together if you would find this helpful. I do hope that you are okay, I always worry about you when we haven't spoken for a long time.

Love,

Lois

January 1993   London

Dear Lois,

Many thanks for your letter. It is good to know that you have finally got stuck into the anthology and are feeling positive about it.

Regarding my piece of writing, you are quite right I can't bear to think about it – though don't think for one moment that I feel hassled by you. My problem is that the arthritis is extremely bad at the present time which means that my reserves are very very low indeed.

Nonetheless I shall attempt to say here what I feel to be the difference between the cancer and the arthritis and it is twofold. One – I suspect this is personal to me – is the pain, which I have yet to experience with the cancer. The arthritic pain is overwhelming me and threatens to do so increasingly and, more to the point, over a long period of time. With the cancer I envisaged a very painful period which would mark the terminal stage at which point I would be offered pain control of whatever cocktail necessary. And I would die. Long-term, non-life-threatening pain sufferers are not so lucky, they are expected to go on for years enduring at best a very inadequate form of pain control. I have suffered enough of the pain to know that 'quality of life' becomes a laughable concept. I am irritable and tearful in turns with fewer and fewer interludes of manic activity when the pain subsides and I attempt to get on with my life.

The second difference links with the first but is in some ways even more painful and that is how one comes to be defined publicly, socially quite simply as a burden. Over and over again in media coverage of 'invalids' the overwhelming emphasis is on the carers and *their* burden, *their* difficulties. No voice is given to the 'invalids' – the complexity of their relationship to their families or loved ones – and it acknowledges nothing of what they are still able to offer which is needed and necessary to those around them. The assumption is that carers have wasted lives, are overburdened, are saints sacrificing themselves to this non-being.

The thought of my relationship with Pete and Charlotte and friends slowly but inexorably being eroded by this dehumanising of what I am, what I mean and what I might continue to be is literally more than I can bear. To be rendered physically helpless is terrifying in itself but the prospect of this continuing for years, to know that I will be in pain, but above all to know that gradually people will see only my physical state is, for me, like being buried alive.

With the cancer, I was clear when I was offered treatment that my major concern would be maintaining quality of life and that was respected. With the arthritis that choice does not exist and, unless I take my own life, I could spend years in a society that does not wish to hear my voice or acknowledge there are other things about me which make me lovable and loving. I don't want to reach a stage where people are happy to tell me how lucky I am to have Pete but no longer believe that he is lucky to have me. Nor do I want all that I have meant to Charlotte and all that she has meant to me to be reduced to the image of invalid mother, put-upon daughter. None of us can survive such images of ourselves.

So, dear Lois, this is as far as I can go with this, whatever energy I have left must be devoted to making my film *Siblings*. I am sorry if you feel I have let you down, but I really am struggling.

Hope all is well with the family and that you remain in good health. It would be nice to see each other just to chat??!

Lots of love to you,

Ellie

5 February 1993   London

My dear Ellie,

I have been thinking about you and your letter all week. I felt that I had been insensitive and silly and also, because we haven't really been in touch for such a long time, that I hadn't been aware of your pain and what is going on in your life. There are a lot of things that I want to say to you so I'll try and put them in some sort of order. I hope this doesn't seem like I am writing you an essay. I am typing this because I have finally reached the point I never thought would happen to me where I write quicker and think more clearly when I am working on the computer.

Firstly about your writing, 'The Visit', which you sent me way back last spring. I have asked myself why it was so important to me that you brought the issue of cancer into this piece and what prevented me from looking at it as a very good piece of writing in its own right. I suppose in my own defence it stemmed from talks we had then about Charlotte and how you had been able to talk to her openly about your cancer but found it surprisingly difficult to talk to her about your escalating arthritis and your fears about becoming disabled. This I suppose was all very near to my own heart, perhaps too near for me to be able to separate my needs as the editor of this book and my personal needs as someone who has had to live with other people's tragedy models about disability and cancer. Cancer has killed the people I love, my brother, mother and father within eight years, and in that sense is indeed a tragedy, but my own paraplegia is something I live with, mostly happily.

One of the hardest things for me when my mum died was the feeling that everyone was looking at me as the third tragedy in this very tragic family and the worst of this was the thought that my dad looked at me this way too. I could say much more about this here and perhaps we will talk about it at some time although I suspect that that would not be very constructive for you. What I want to say here is that your piece of writing is good and complete. It tells its own story and I should have had the sense to realise long ago that this is what you want to write and this is what you have written. At the moment I am collecting work together for a rather long shortlist and will make final decisions when I have discussed it with my own editor from The Women's Press. With your permission, I have put 'The Visit' on that list.

The next thing I want to say is that I want to offer my empathy (can you offer empathy?) with what you say about your feelings about being defined publicly as a burden. This is something I have lived with since my accident although for me this has become easier over the last few years as the social circumstances of my life have enabled me to be less dependent and I have become more confident about who I am and where I am prepared to ask for and receive help. For you this is new and raw and is getting worse.

I can only say that I hope you will find me a safe place where you can share some of these things. It is very important that we (and by this I mean disabled people, although I don't know how you feel about me including you here) don't create a hierarchy for ourselves. We share a lot of things about our own fears, about redefining independence and partnership and about dealing with how the world outside sees us. I have sent you a copy of an article I wrote for an academic journal after a series of seminars I was involved with. It's a bit dry and lengthy but it does talk about some of the things you say in your letter.

And that brings me on to the last thing I want to write about: pain. Oh God, Ellie, it's awful for you, and no, I haven't shared this and I don't know what it must be like except that it must be unbearable sometimes. I hope that there are times you can still be your same old strong, funny, beautiful Ellie and that you will find someone who can find a way to help control the pain. I also want to say that through this book I am in touch with a number of women who have rheumatoid arthritis. One woman who has had this condition since she was small has sent me the first eight chapters of her book and I have spoken to her on the phone. She is about thirty, I think, and very nice. If you would like to talk to her I could put you in touch.

That's it for now. Despite what you said, you obviously did feel that I had not really understood what was going on for you and you were right. I didn't feel that I could talk to you properly again until we had sorted some of this out. I hope we can now.

With much love,

Lois

11 February 1993   London

Dear, dear Lois,

I feel like I have been in free fall for the last few months and then your letter arrived and for this blissful moment I felt held. It isn't that everyone hasn't tried to catch me, it is rather that in having no experience of my situation they haven't known how to, and often their efforts have only added to the pain. So my sense of isolation has been increasing and your lovely letter has reminded me that I am not completely alone with this thing – that others know what it is like too.

Your article (which arrived in the same post as the letter) covered everything I have been feeling recently. As you say, one doesn't want to deny the importance of the carer. Pete couldn't have been more loving or patient – but it has felt as if overnight my status as invalid or disabled has obliterated the rest of who I am. I don't know where that sense of things is born, Pete certainly doesn't view it in this way, maybe it has come only from me. The growing sense of helplessness has been terrifying, bewildering and I haven't known who to turn to.

My GP is lovely but the drugs she has given me haven't really dealt with the pain and my 'emergency' appointment with the rheumatologist will not be until March 10th, eight weeks time. Can you imagine? I would love, therefore, to be put in touch with the woman you mentioned in your letter who has lived with rheumatoid arthritis since she was small. She must have controlled the pain somehow. If I could get the pain under control I do think I could cope with the disability, really I do.

But your letter did offer me such hope, Lois. I can't think why I haven't sought to approach other disabled people. I think the true madness is that I don't think of you as disabled because I too have that model in my head of what it means, i.e. 'passive, helpless and demanding', which you are not, but which I have felt myself to be recently.

So maybe if I can talk to people with my condition who have found a way of living with the disease I can find some encouragement which I definitely need at the moment.

I am continuing with *Siblings* which raises other pains and hurts and as I said to you in my last letter, I am making it a do or die number.

Lastly, a million thanks for considering 'The Visit' for your shortlist. I do understand your wanting me to deal with the cancer too but I think you identified the problem yourself, cancer is a tragedy giving the sufferer their due place, disability doesn't do that. Worse, it threatens to separate me from Pete and Charlotte by making them 'carers' and me burden. One is supposed to care for one's child, not be cared for by them.

No, that doesn't explain it either. I'll have to keep on trying.

I want Pete to post this letter now so I'll have to leave it. I want you to have this before I speak to you on the phone, I'll ring you in a couple of weeks. You really have made me feel so much better. I want to thank you for that. Take care, Lois. After this I have forgotten to ask you how you are except your letter suggests all is well for which I am glad.

Lots of love to you,

Ellie

Contributors' Notes

ASPEN is a disabled lesbian, passionate about life, love, friendship and positive change. She has written poetry, stories and articles for publication since the seventies although illness has seriously held up her output. A member of lesbianspirit writing group, she is now also working on a novel. She hopes other disabled women will write about their lives.

RUTH BAILEY is 31 and lives happily in North London, surrounded by plants, books and music. She works and studies part-time and enjoys ruminating with friends on the many meanings of life.

CAROLINE BALL has cerebral palsy. Born in Africa in 1953, she lived with her family abroad and at home and then for many years in residential care. She has recently moved into a bungalow in the community. Three years ago she joined a disabled writers' group and has had her work read on the radio and published by Commonword. She loves dogs.

ELSA BECKETT is 54, paraplegic, lesbian. Born in Africa, she has lived with her partner in Britain since 1969. She works on committees of local disability and lesbian/gay groups but her main voluntary commitment is to Gemma, the national group of lesbians and bisexual women with/without disability. She has had many short stories published and is currently working on a novel dealing with disability and sexuality.

NASA BEGUM is a black disabled woman who is actively involved in the struggles and celebrations of many movements. She is employed as a project co-director with Living Options Partnership to promote the involvement of people in service development. Her publications include *Burden of Gratitude* (1989) and *Something to be Proud of* (1992). Nasa spends the rest of her time plotting the revolution at grassroots level. She loves demos, shopping, other people's parties and being with friends.

KATE BROMFIELD is a teacher, a writer, and a supporter of Amnesty International and CND. She loves music, art, the theatre and experimenting with traditional crafts. She began to write seriously in 1992 and has had her work shortlisted in two competitions. She is working on her first collection of short stories and a children's book. She shares a house in South London with her husband, two children, a cat and a guinea pig.

MERRY CROSS is a long-time disability activist who does not like to be pigeon-holed. She has been a teacher, psychologist, actress, writer and disability equality trainer, and has worked with disabled children in Kenya. Now, at the age of 42, she has produced wonderful twin girls of mixed race. She runs a disability consultancy and is hoping to offer psychotherapy counselling to abused, disabled children.

LIZ CROW is a disabled feminist who has been active in the Disabled People's Movement for the past decade. Since 1987 she has worked as a disability equality consultant, particularly in the education, arts and media and health sectors. Published writing includes 'Renewing the Social Model of Disability' (*Coalition News*), 'On Our Own Terms' (*Women's Art*), 'A Divided Island' (*Nothing Ventured: Disabled People Travel The World*) and 'Photography and Disability' (Arts Council). Liz's piece in this book is based on letters written to her sister Judith who lives in California.

CELESTE DANDEKER was born in 1951, her parents' fourth child. After leaving boarding school, she moved to London to train in contemporary dance and to discover the swinging sixties. During a short but exciting dance career she became quadraplegic after falling on stage. Rediscovering dance in 1990, she co-founded CandoCo Dance Company. Life has not been the same since. Celeste lives independently in North London with the help of a personal assistant.

MARY DUFFY is 32 years old and has been working as an artist for almost ten years. She is a photographer and writer and performs her own work as well as doing a variety of part-time jobs. She has just completed a master's degree in Equality Studies in the hope of getting a Real Job. She lives with her partner in Bray, County Wicklow, in the Republic of Ireland.

SALLY FRENCH was born in 1949 with a severe visual impairment. She worked for four years as a physiotherapist in Britain and abroad but is now a lecturer, writer and perpetual student. She currently works for The Open University and has written books on many subjects including research, medical sociology, the art of writing and disability studies.

JENI FULTON is a 37-year-old disabled woman with a well-developed sense of the absurd, strong red-green political instincts, and a passion for her friends, family, the sea and words (not necessarily in that order). She co-exists, sometimes happily, with a career in public sector services, but tries to leave enough energy for exercising her pen/word processor and her imagination.

EVE GOSS was born and bred in the West of England in the twenties and thirties. An eye impairment hindered her early career as a reporter and civil servant but she qualified as an interpreter at the Geneva Interpreters' School and taught English in six countries, sometimes with the British Council. She lives in Hampstead where she brought up her disabled son and fought accidents and illness as well as campaigning. She loves laughter, music, truth, kindness, clean air and water and fights for a fair, tolerant society.

MILLEE HILL was born in 1957 in Bermuda but was brought up in America and Canada. She broke her neck in a diving accident when she was fourteen. She was a professional journalist for a number of years, has a degree in law and is now doing postgraduate study with a view to becoming a practising barrister. She is the co-founder of the Black Disabled People's Group which was set up to address the problem of under-representation of Black people in society in general and within the disability movement.

MOLLY HOLDEN was born in London in 1927 but lived most of her life in the country and these landscapes were the source of much of her poetry. She married in 1949 and had two children. In 1954, she developed the first symptoms of multiple sclerosis. In the following years she began to write, and her poems were published to critical acclaim. Many of them are about what she describes as 'the feelings and reactions of a young woman whose life was drastically changed'. She died in 1981. A selected edition of the poems of Molly Holden is available from Carcanet Press (1987).

JENNIFER HOSKINS was born in 1967. She graduated in computing and astronomy from the Hatfield Polytechnic in 1988 and hasn't yet had many poems published. She currently lives in Reading and enjoys drawing, making lemon cheese cake, Blu-Tacking poems to walls, co-counselling and putting the kettle on. Disabled by Myalgic Encephalomyelitis, she runs a support group and is enthusiastic about the disability civil rights movement.

MARIA JASTRZEBSKA was born in Warsaw, Poland, in 1953. She is the author of *Postcards From Poland and other correspondences* (Working Press) with artist Jola Scicińska, and co-editor of the *Forum Polek – Polish Women's Forum Anthology*. She has taught women's self-defence, is a lesbian and lives by the seaside with a proverbially wonderful cat. She has ME, Myalgic Encephalomyelitis, aka CFIDS, Chronic Fatigue Immune Dysfunction Syndrome.

LOIS KEITH was born in 1950. She now lives in London with her family and teaches English part-time in an inner city comprehensive school. She writes, edits and spends a lot of time talking to friends on the telephone for the rest of the working week. She has recently written two books on English teaching published by Longman/BBC Enterprises as well as a variety of bits, pieces and poems on disability issues.

HELEN KENDALL is 46 and lives in Bath. She teaches for the Health Service and writes publicity material for the Cancer and Leukaemia in Childhood Trust (CLIC). Three cats, a very good friend with whom she lives, two delightful grown-up sons, walking, and studying for an MA in creative writing fill up most of the rest of her life.

DIANE KENYON was born with partial hearing but is now severely deaf. She is a freelance lecturer, tutor and writer on deafness and is particularly interested in the subject of being a deaf parent. She has presented the LINK programme for disabled people and in 1972 helped to found the BREAKTHROUGH self-help movement, administered by deaf people. She is married to a profoundly deaf person.

GOHAR KORDI was born in Iran to a peasant family. She became blind at the age of three and as there were no schools for blind girls in Tehran, she did not start her education until she was 14. She was the first blind woman to enter the University of Tehran where she took a BA degree in Psychology. She moved to England in 1971. Her story 'From Missionary School to Mitcham' appeared in a collection *So Very English* and her autobiographical novel *An Iranian Odyssey* was published in the same year (Serpent's Tail, 1991). Her second book is published by The Women's Press and Gohar is currently working on a stage play and a third novel. She has written a film script based on her life for BBC 2. She lives in London with her husband and her ten-year-old son.

ANN MACFARLANE, a wheelchair user, is self-employed as a disability equality training consultant. She is involved in the disability movement and is on the Independent Living Sub-Group of the British Council of Organisations of Disabled People (BCODP). Ann has been instrumental in establishing two organisations of disabled people. She is an author and poet and her work includes writing about cookery, poems and articles in *Community Care*, *Nursing Mirror* and *Social Work Today*. She is an elder in the United Reformed Church and has no desire to be 'cured'.

JAIHN MAKAYUTE, Incarnate since 7.6.62. Disabled since 25.9.87. She experienced many – including spinal – wounds. The healing continues: she moves on; Lovelearning, still. Awakening to the marvels of Being. She paints beauty on to silk and she spins webs with words. *Caduceus*, *Resurgence*, and *Kindred Spirit* magazines have printed her poems. 'Freedom Fighter' is part of her forthcoming book: *FreeWheelinto Ancient Newness*, the publisher for which she is currently magnetising.

PAM MASON was born in Liverpool in 1961. She attended Roby Comprehensive School and the University of East Anglia and has worked on a magazine and at an arts centre. She has had work published in *Spare Rib* and *Everywoman* and short stories broadcast by Radio Merseyside. At present she is working on a novel about sectarianism.

JENNI MEREDITH succumbed to epileptic seizures through-out her fine art course in the late 1960s and now spends more time writing than drawing. She has published poems, articles and cartoons, including four poems in the anthology *The Bees Sneeze*

(Stride, 1992). She lives in the Isle of Wight with her artist husband and their 23-year-old son who is a juggler and clown. They work together on music and writing projects for local schools. Jenni is co-ordinator of a postal writing forum of disabled people, Write to Belong.

DOROTHY (DOT) MILES was born in North Wales in 1931. She became deaf from meningitis at the age of eight and attended the Manchester Royal School for the Deaf where she was not known as Dot but as 152. Sign language was forbidden in schools at that time but amongst her friends, Dot was a great storyteller. In America she studied at the Gallaudet College, at the time the only college for the deaf, and later wrote *A Play of Our Own*, the first play about deaf people to be performed in sign language all over the world. Her work and research shaped the thinking of deaf and hearing people in the fields of sign language, theatre and poetry. Dot died in 1993.

JENNY MORRIS is 43 years old and shares her house with her 11-year-old daughter. For a number of years she taught housing and sociology at a college of further education, and she now writes and does a variety of freelance work around disability issues. Her publications include *Able Lives: Women's Experience of Paralysis* (The Women's Press, 1989); *Pride Against Prejudice: Transforming Attitudes to Disability* (The Women's Press, 1991); *Alone Together: Voices of Single Mothers* (The Women's Press, 1992); and *Independent Lives? Community Care and Disabled People* (Macmillan, 1993).

KAITE O'REILLY writes primarily for theatre and radio. As a performer she toured nationally and went to Malaysia with GræÆ Theatre Company. She is involved with various organisations run by disabled people teaching performance and creative writing. Currently writing her first novel, she lectures in theatre and media drama at the University of Glamorgan.

ELLIE O'SULLIVAN, born in 1947, is an independent film

maker currently working on her third film, *Siblings*. Her first film, *A Place Away* (1989), was shortlisted for the Holstein Export Short Film Award at the Piccadilly Festival 1990. Her second, *Family Album*, was broadcast on Channel 4 in December 1992. She is a director of Local Radio Workshop where she runs courses in sound recording in exchange for the use of workshop facilities to edit her film soundtracks. She lives in London with her family. She has had rheumatoid arthritis since 1970 and was diagnosed with breast cancer in 1981 with a recurrence in 1986.

EMILY OXFORD is 32 and has had juvenile arthritis since the age of two. She has been a singer and performer of all types of music but her main interest is writing. Under various guises, she writes when she can on all topics, and has had work published in many outlets including *Disability Arts Magazine* where she was film columnist for a year. She was the main author of *Our Relationships, Our Sexuality*, for people with arthritis. She sees her impairment as an integrated, valid (if sometimes painful) part of herself. She lives on the edge of Epping Forest with her partner Andy and her three elderly cats.

JANICE PINK is a lesbian in her fifties, living in London with two dogs and three cats. Long and happily divorced, she has three grown-up children. She has had articles and poems published in *DAIL* magazine and in various newsletters, and is working on a novel. As well as writing, she is addicted to the grandchildren, cups of tea and *Prisoner: Cell Block H*.

SUNA POLIO was lucky enough to miss the Second World War but be in time for the sixties, the women's liberation movement and the disabled people's movement. Having had polio at the age of seven, she is still finding lots to learn about disability. She became a parent three years ago, and this has opened up new worlds of love, play and delight, as well as heaping on extra dollops of oppression. She lives in the North of England with her lover and their child, and is planning to knock some more holes in her home to improve its accessibility.

DIANE PUNGARTNIK is an American actress and cabaret artist with epilepsy who lives in London. All offers of work are very welcome.

ROZ RUSHWORTH was born in London in 1933 and has written about her experiences as an evacuee. She has four grown-up children and seven grandchildren. She lives with her husband and chihuahua, Kissy, in a tranquil setting by a wood in Yorkshire. She enjoys writing, performing, loves to sing and is learning to play the keyboard.

ANNA SULLIVAN was born in 1939 in the East End of London. She left school at 16 and had the first of her three children in 1959. After twelve years at home, she did a teaching degree and taught in Islington schools until she became disabled and had to retire in 1989. She brought up her family mostly as a single parent and has been an active trade unionist and anti-fascist campaigner most of her adult life. Her poetry has been published in *Poetry Now* (1994) and shortlisted for the London Writers Competition. She now lives happily alone and spends her time painting and writing, enjoying her grandchildren and the conversation of friends.

MICHELE WATES was diagnosed as having MS over ten years ago, since when she has had two children. She is spokesperson for ParentAbility, supporting the rights of disabled people as parents, and is assembling a picture collection which she hopes will dispel the myth that disabled people do not have children. She has co-written a booklet for Women's Health, *Disabled Mothers – Supporting Each Other*, and is currently writing a book based on interviews with disabled parents.